Study Guide for

AFTER THE TRADE IS MADE

An Operations Training Manual

ABOUT THE PUBLISHER

The New York Institute of Finance

. . . more than just books.

NYIF offers practical, applied education and training in a wide range of financial topics:

* *Classroom training:* evenings, mornings, noon-hour
* *Seminars:* one- and two-day professional and introductory programs
* *Customized training:* need-specific, on your site or ours, in New York City, throughout the United States, anywhere in the world
* *Independent study:* self-paced learning—basic, intermediate, advanced
* *Exam preparation:* NASD licensing (including Series 7), CFA prep, state life and health insurance licensing

Subjects of books and training programs include the following:

* *Account Executive Training*
* *Brokerage Operations*
* *Futures Trading*
* *International Corporate Finance*
* *Options as a Strategic Investment*
* *Securities Transfer*
* *Technical Analysis*

*When Wall Street professionals think **training**, they think **NYIF**.*

Please write or call for our catalog:

New York Institute of Finance
70 Pine Street
New York, NY 10270–0003
212 / 344–2900

Simon & Schuster, Inc. A Gulf + Western Company

"Where Wall Street Goes to School" tm

Study Guide for

AFTER THE TRADE IS MADE

An Operations Training Manual

The New York Institute of Finance

New York Institute of Finance

Library of Congress Cataloging-in-Publication Data

Study guide for After the trade is made.

"Designed for use with David M. Weiss's After the trade is made: processing securities."—

1. Weiss, David M., 1938– . After the trade is made. 2. Stock-exchange—United States. 3. Securities—United States. 4. Commodity exchanges—United States.
I. New York Institute of Finance. II. Weiss, David M.,
1938– . After the trade is made.
HG4910.W365 1986 332.64'273 87–14155
ISBN 0–13–858721–3

A D'Maracra Product

This publication is designed to provide accurate and authoritative information in regard to the subject matter covered. It is sold with the understanding that the publisher is not engaged in rendering legal, accounting, or other professional service. If legal advice or other expert assistance is required, the services of a competent professional person should be sought.

From a Declaration of Principles Jointly Adopted by a Committee of the American Bar Association and a Committee of Publishers and Associations

Printed in the United States of America

10 9 8 7 6 5 4 3 2 1

New York Institute of Finance
(NYIF Corp.)
70 Pine Street
New York, NY 10270-0003

How to Use This Guide

This self-study workbook as been designed for use with David M. Weiss's *After the Trade Is Made: Processing Securities Transactions.* Its aim is to enable you to take a course in operations procedures at your own pace and in a cost-effective way.

To begin, turn to page 1 of this guide. There you will find a Reading Assignment, Objectives, Reading Orientation, and Key Terms. The Reading Assignment is a section of the text, *After the Trade Is Made*. Before reading the assignment, however, review the key terms. You will find these terms in the assigned section of the text. Pay special attention to these terms.

Once you have read the assignment, making marginal notes and underlining in the text, turn to the Challenge section of the lesson, which contains a Matching Quiz, True/False, Multiple Choice questions, and sometimes Fill-Ins. Answer these questions to the best of your ability *closed book*—that is, do not refer back to the text to find the answers. Then grade yourself by checking your answers against those provided on the Answer Sheet at the very end of the lesson. Each question is assigned a point value, so that you can arrive at a grade.

The purpose of self-grading is to evaluate your comprehension of the reading assignment. If your grade totals less than 65 in any lesson, you should go back to the assigned section, reread it (or at least the parts you did not understand), and then go back to the questions until you understand the correct answer.

Do this for each lesson.

The purpose of this guide is not—and cannot be—to train you in your firm's procedures. Rather, it is to give you a detailed understanding of:

- The functions of various operations departments.
- The relationships among those departments.
- Regulatory requirements.
- The language of operations.

With these basics, you are prepared to better understand and utilize *your firm's* methods, procedures, and terminology. You are on your way to becoming a skilled and informed operations professional.

Contents

Study Guide for

AFTER THE TRADE IS MADE

An Operations Training Manual

LESSON ONE

Underwritings

READING ASSIGNMENT

Chapter 1 Underwritings: The Birth of a Security
Chapter 2 Other Types of Underwritings

OBJECTIVES

- To distinguish between the primary forms of business ownership: proprietorship, partnership, corporation.
- To understand the various forms and functions of underwriting.
- To comprehend security issuance.

READING ORIENTATION

The first two chapters of the text introduce you to the various forms of *underwriting*. This is the process by which securities are first brought to the market or offered for sale to the public.

Once you understand how the business sector of the economy is broken down according to ownership, then the details involving issuance of its securities will become clearer.

Securities are issued by corporations, municipalities, mutual funds, the U.S. government, and also by the public.

KEY TERMS

All-or-none, 19
Best efforts underwriting, 18–19
Bond, 7
Cooling-off period, 11
Corporation, 5–6
Municipalities, 19–20
Mutual fund, 22–23
Partnership, 4
Pre-emptive right, 17
Preliminary prospectus, 7–9
Private sector, 16
Proprietorship, 4
Red herring, 7–9
Spread, 13
Stabilizing the market, 12
Standby underwriting, 18
State of incorporation, 16
Stock, 6–7
Syndicate, 7–9
Underwriting, 3, 6

Challenge

MATCHING QUIZ

Match each term at the left with a definition at the right, by placing the number of the definition in the fill-in space next to the term. There are more definitions than terms. (Each question is worth 2 points.)

_____ **limited partner**

_____ **spread**

_____ **corporation**

_____ **proprietorship**

_____ **general partner**

_____ **shareholder**

_____ **cooling-off period**

_____ **red herring**

_____ **preferred stock**

_____ **pre-emptive rights**

_____ **mutual fund**

_____ **underwriting**

_____ **syndicate**

1. Process by which securities are first brought to the market.

2. Represents ownership in the issuing corporation, with receipt of dividends before all others.

3. Partner who shares in management decisions.

4. The difference between what the issuer receives and what the security sells for.

5. A pool of money used for specific investment purposes.

6. Partner without any voice in management or policy-making decisions.

7. Preliminary prospectus.

8. Simplest form of business.

9. Stockholder maintains percentage of ownership in the corporation before additional stock can be issued.

10. Life of the business is separate from that of the owners.

11. SEC reviews registration statement.

12. Liability limited to investment.

13. A registration statement.

14. Means of stabilizing the market.

15. Group of brokerage firms that will guarantee, or underwrite, the sale of a new issue.

MULTIPLE CHOICE

Select the letter that best answers the numbered question. (Each question is worth 5 points.)

1. The ability of a single proprietor to raise funds is based on the worth of the:

a) individual
b) business
c) shareholders
d) limited partners
e) all of the above

2. A general partner is responsible for paying what portion of the partnership debt?

a) one share
b) all
c) up to their portion of ownership
d) up to their investment
e) one half

3. A limited partner may be which of the following?

a) part of management
b) an investor in the company
c) responsible for ½ of the debts
d) a and c only
e) a, b, and c

4. The ability of a partnership to raise capital is dependent on the:

a) value of entity
b) worth of the individuals
c) business outlook
d) value of the common shares
e) dividends paid

5. The form of business recognized as an individual under law is:

a) proprietorship
b) partnership
c) corporation
d) syndicate
e) all of the above

6. The formal document used to attract other firms into the underwriting is known as the:

a) final prospectus
b) book of forms
c) preliminary prospectus
d) offering circular
e) book offering

7. The form used to obtain SEC permission to issue the security to the public is the:

a) red herring
b) blue skying
c) registration statement
d) primary prospectus
e) Reg T form

Questions 8–10 concern an underwriting of 1,000,000 shares of ZAP. There is one manager, Stone, Forrest & Rivers. Including SF&R, there are five underwriters. Including the five underwriters there are 10 firms selling the stock to their customers. ZAP will be paid $9.00 per share, and the offering will be made to the public at $10.00 per share. The manager will receive $.10 per share as the fee. Each underwriter will receive $.15 for each share underwritten and each of the 10 firms selling receive $.75 per share for each share they sell.

8. Stone, Forrest & Rivers is the underwriting manager of 1,000,000 shares. How much of a fee will SF&R receive as manager?

- **a)** $9,000,000
- **b)** $10,000,000
- **c)** $100,000
- **d)** $750,000
- **e)** $75,000

9. Giant Recker & Crane underwrote 200,000 shares of ZAP. The underwriting fee on this portion is:

- **a)** $75,000
- **b)** $30,000
- **c)** $100,000
- **d)** $900,000
- **e)** $1,800,000

10. The form of underwriting under which the underwriter does not buy (take down) the new issue, but accepts the deal without exposure is:

- **a)** competitive
- **b)** negotiated
- **c)** standby
- **d)** cooling off
- **e)** all-or-none

TRUE/FALSE

Questions 11-22 are either true or false. Mark T for true, F for false. (Each question is worth 2 points.)

11. An individual who does not want his/her involvement with a partnership known is a limited partner. ______

12. A proprietorship continues from owner to owner. ______

13. Partnership agreements must be approved by the Secretary of a State. ______

14. Most corporate issues are brought to market through a form of underwriting known as negotiated underwriting. ______

15. A form of debt that a corporation may issue is preferred stock. ______

16. The red herring is a final prospectus. ______

17. Firms that assist in the distribution of the new issue but do not participate in the underwriting are known as the selling group. ______

18. The clause in a corporate charter that gives present share-owners the ability to purchase additional shares before nonshare-holders can acquire them is known as preemptive rights. ______

19. Municipal securities are usually brought to market through a negotiated underwriting. ______

20. Government securities are issued by state or local governments. ______

21. Issues comprised of the pooling of money to achieve a particular goal are known as futures. ______

22. The preliminary prospectus contains all the terms of the underwriting. ______

Answer Sheet

Matching Quiz

6 limited partner
4 spread
10 corporation
8 proprietorship
3 general partner
12 shareholder
11 cooling-off period
7 red herring
2 preferred stock
9 pre-emptive rights
5 mutual fund
1 underwriting
15 syndicate

Multiple Choice

1. a
2. b
3. b
4. b
5. c
6. c
7. c
8. c
9. b
10. c

True/False

11. F
12. F
13. F
14. T
15. F
16. F
17. T
18. T
19. F
20. F
21. F
22. F

LESSON TWO

The Over-the-Counter Market and the Exchanges

READING ASSIGNMENT

Chapter 3 The Over-the-Counter (OTC) Market
Chapter 4 The Exchanges

OBJECTIVES

- To understand the function, nature, and policies of the over-the-counter market.
- To identify the different types of exchanges.
- To describe the difference between the NYSE and the AMEX.

READING ORIENTATION

When a security issues comes to market, the public has the opportunity to own the security. The means of doing so is provided by the over-the-counter market and the various exchanges. The marketplace where securities are bought and sold is where it all happens.

General information about the marketplace is discussed in this lesson's reading assignment. Though the description is brief compared to other texts, this degree of detail is sufficient for your current needs.

KEY TERMS

Block-trading firm, 46
Blue list, 27
Business Conduct Committee, 25
Commission-house broker, 36
Current yield, 29
Dually listed security, 35
Firm quote, 27
Liquidity, 24
Market makers, 25
Mark up, 26
National Association of Securities Dealers (NASD), 25
Nominal yield, 29
Parity, 43
Pink sheets, 27
Precedence, 42
Priority, 41–42
Priority prorata, 45
Registered trader, 40
Round lot, 41–42
Rules of Fair Practice, 25
Short, 32
Specialist, 37, 40
Subject quote, 28
Telephone booth, 40
Trading post, 40
Two-dollar broker, 36–37
Uniform Practice Code, 25
Work-out markets, 28
Yield-to-maturity rate, 29

Challenge

MATCHING QUIZ

Match each term at the left with a definition at the right, by placing the number of the definition in the fill-in space next to the term. There are more definitions than terms. (Each question is worth 2 points.)

______ **agents**

______ **subject quote**

______ **dealer**

______ **specialist**

______ **OBO**

______ **liquidity**

______ **principal**

______ **yield**

______ **regional exchanges**

______ **commission-house broker**

______ **priority**

______ **inventory**

______ **Uniform Practice Code**

1. Maintains fair and orderly markets in stocks assigned to them.

2. Percentage of return on an investment.

3. Individuals who are employed by member firms and who execute orders for their firms' customers.

4. Operates on CBOE.

5. Market maker.

6. Mark up the securities they trade with the public.

7. A quote at which the market maker is willing to trade.

8. MSE, PSE, PHLX, BSE.

9. Price at which the trader believes the trade can be consummated.

10. Determined by the order's time of entry.

11. Ease with which an investor can convert an investment into cash.

12. Establishes procedures utilized in broker/broker or broker/dealer relationships.

13. Quotes for dollar-priced securities.

14. Represents investments of a market maker's firm's capital.

15. Never directly own any inventory.

MULTIPLE CHOICE

Select the letter that best answers the numbered question. (Each question is worth 5 points.)

1. The process by which a corporation brings its common stock to the market for the first time is known as:

a) first offering
b) common stock
c) going public
d) NYSE listing
e) incorporation

2. Corporations bring new securities to the market with the assistance of the:

a) investment banker
b) mortgage banker
c) commercial banker
d) broker/dealer
e) small business administration

3. Which of the following securities trade over-the-counter?

a) common stock
b) preferred stock
c) corporate bonds
d) municipal bonds
e) all of the above

4. The NASD rules that govern broker and customer relationships are known as:

a) B-C rules
b) Rules of Fair Practice
c) Uniform Practice Code
d) Regulation T
e) NYSE Constitution

Questions 5 and 6 refer to the following firm dealer quotes on RAM.

Dealer	*Bid*	*Offer*
A	32	32½
B	32¼	32¾
C	32⅛	32⅝

5. A customer of Stone, Forrest & Rivers wants to purchase 100 shares of RAM at the market. An employee on SF&R's OTC trading desk will call which dealer to execute the order?

a) Dealer A

b) Dealer B

c) Dealer C

6. Suppose the customer in question 5 wanted to sell instead of buy. Which dealer would SF&R's trading desk call to execute the order?

a) Dealer A

b) Dealer B

c) Dealer C

7. Compute the current yield on the following bond:

$1,000 RAM 10% − FA − 2006 = 90 ($900)

The current yield is:

a) 10%

b) 9%

c) 9.26%

d) 11.11%

e) 12.25%

8. Referring to question 7, assume that the purchase year was 1986. What would the yield-to-maturity rate be?

a) 10.5%

b) 11.05%

c) 11.21%

d) 12.25%

e) 9.76%

9. Which of the following are members of the NYSE's equity marketplace?

1. commission-house brokers
2. two-dollar brokers
3. specialists
4. market makers
5. registered traders

a) 1 and 2

b) 1, 3 and 5

c) 1, 2, 3 and 5

d) 1, 2 and 5

e) 3 and 4

10. Bids received on POW, 46 per share, are made in the following time frame: (POW is traded on the NYSE.)

Broker A—100 shares at 1:12 P.M.
Broker B—300 shares at 1:13 P.M.
Broker C—400 shares at 1:14 P.M.
Broker D—800 shares at 1:15 P.M.

Broker "X" enters the "crowd" at 1:16 P.M. with a sell 800 shares. The order would be filled as follows:

a) Broker A—100, Broker C—300, Broker D—400 shares.

b) Broker A—100, Broker B—200, Broker C—200, Broker D—300 shares.

c) Broker A—100, Broker D—700 shares.

d) Broker D—800 shares.

e) Broker C—200, Broker D—600 shares.

TRUE/FALSE

Questions 11–22 are either true or false. Mark T for true, F for false. (Each question is worth 2 points.)

11. The OTC market is governed by the NASD. ______

12. NASD firms, in dealing with each other, must adhere to the NASD Uniform Practice Code. ______

13. Another name for basis price is current yield. ______

14. Another name for market maker is dealer. ______

15. A two-dollar broker, on the floor of the NYSE, executes orders for the public customers of his firm. ______

16. On the NYSE, stocks trade at booths. ______

17. Over-the-counter stock prices can be found in a publication known as the blue list. ______

18. Securities that are not traded over-the-counter are listed and traded on exchanges. ______

19. An order that can best fill the quote takes parity. ______

20. The procedure on the AMEX for awarding trades is known as priority prorata. ______

21. Large-quantity trades are handled by block-trading firms. ______

22. A fair and orderly market is maintained by the registered trader. ______

Answer Sheet

Matching Quiz

15 agents
9 subject quote
5 dealer
1 specialist
4 OBO
11 liquidity
6 principal
2 yield
8 regional exchanges
3 commission-house broker
10 priority
14 inventory
12 Uniform Practice Code

Multiple Choice

1. c
2. a
3. e
4. b
5. a
6. b
7. d
8. b
9. c
10. c

True/False

11. T
12. T
13. F
14. T
15. F
16. F
17. F
18. T
19. F
20. T
21. T
22. F

LESSON THREE

Operations: The Order Room and the Purchase and Sales Department

READING ASSIGNMENT

Chapter 5 Operations: A Comparison
Chapter 6 Order Room
Chapter 7 Purchase and Sales (P&S)

OBJECTIVES

- To understand the organization of a brokerage firm.
- To be able to reproduce a general flowchart of a typical operations organization.
- To identify types of orders.
- To explain the responsibilities of the Purchase and Sales department.

READING ORIENTATION

The three chapters covered in this lesson begin to describe the details of operations. The organization of a brokerage firm is introduced, as well as the functions of some of the processing areas.

The *order room* is where processing begins for all orders. The employees are responsible for controlling, servicing, maintaining, and recording the execution of all orders directed to them.

The next step is the *purchase and sales* (P&S) function. This includes computing the amount of money involved in the trade, making certain that the opposing brokerage firm agrees with the terms of the transaction, and balancing customer and brokerage trades.

KEY TERMS

Accrued interest, 64
All-or-none, 57
Balance, 67
Blotter, 66
Booking, 70
Branches, 51
Code, 62
Combination order, 58
Comparison, 66
Confirmation, 68
Contract sheets, 67
Execution report, 59
Figuration, 64
Fill-or-kill, 57
Good-til-cancelled, 58
Immediate or cancel, 57
Limit order, 57
Market order, 55
Marketing/sales function, 51
One cancels other, 58
Pending orders, 59
Product mix, 51
Reconcile, 58
Spread order, 58
Stop order, 57
Stop limit, 57
Straddle order, 58
Ticket, 62
Uncompared, 67

Challenge

MATCHING QUIZ

Match each term at the left with a definition at the right, by placing the number of the definition in the fill-in space next to the term. There are more definitions than terms. (Each question is worth 1 point.)

_____ **limit order**

_____ **comparison**

_____ **FOK**

_____ **market order**

_____ **confirmation**

_____ **AON**

_____ **stop**

_____ **figuration**

_____ **product mix**

_____ **code**

_____ **blotter**

_____ **clearing corporation**

_____ **booking**

_____ **contract sheet**

_____ **CUSIP**

1. Responsible for auditing a trade.

2. Firm-to-customer correspondence.

3. Identifies the issuer and issue on a trade.

4. Entering the trade in the firm's records.

5. Designates the type of transaction.

6. A memorandum order.

7. A receipt and distribution center—NSCC.

8. Firm-to-firm correspondence.

9. A short sale.

10. Listing of trade information from both buyer and seller firms.

11. Trade listing.

12. The combination of types of securities that a firm offers its customers.

13. Sets highest price to pay or lowest price to receive.

14. Accepts current price.

15. Customer-monies computation.

16. Must be executed in its entirety immediately.

17. All of the order must be filled.

MULTIPLE CHOICE

Select the letter that best answers the numbered question. (Each question is worth 4 points.)

1. The responsibility for control and monitoring of customer orders is:

a) order room
b) P&S
c) margin
d) cashiers
e) stock record

2. The department responsible for trade figuration is the:

a) order room
b) P&S
c) margin
d) cashiers
e) stock record

3. Wynn Doe purchases a corporate bond $1,000 RAM 9% JJ (January 1 and July 1)—2006 at 93. The trade date is April 9, and the settlement date is April 16. How many days of accrued interest should be accounted for?

a) 105
b) 106
c) 16
d) 15
e) 90

4. Which of the following must be on a customer's confirmation?

I. bought or sold
II. quantity and price
III. security description
IV. trade date and settlement date
V. place of execution

a) I, II, IV
b) I, II, III
c) III, IV, V
d) I, III, V
e) I, II, III, IV, V

5. Stockbrokers work in offices known as:

a) closets
b) branches
c) booths
d) order room
e) banks

6. Ralph Michaels buys 100 shares of RAM at $55 per share. Because he does not want to risk more than $500 on this transaction, he enters an order to sell 100 RAM at 50 stop. Before this order can be executed, what must take place?

a) the market must go up at least 5 points
b) he must buy another 100 shares
c) the market must close for the day
d) the market must fall to 50 or below
3) a straddle order must be placed

7. What is another term for the computation of trades?

a) figuration
b) reconcilement
c) ordering
d) comparison
e) all of the above

8. Orders that stay "open" until they are executed or the customer enters a cancel are:

a) OCO
b) IOC
c) FOK
d) AON
e) GTC

9. An order entered in the marketplace is executed. Notification of the execution that is received by the account executive is known as a:

a) pending
b) report
c) marketing
d) functional
e) bid

10. When P&S receives a listing of all broker trades that were processed the day before but executed two days earlier, what day is this?

a) blotter day
b) trade date
c) trade date + 1
d) trade date + 2
e) trade date + 3

11. Clearing organizations issue:

a) blotters
b) balance sheets
c) contract sheets
d) bonds
e) tickets

TRUE/FALSE

Questions 12–25 are either true of false. Mark T for true, F for false. (Each question is worth 3 points.)

12. The order that remains in force until it is executed or cancelled is a limit order. ______

13. An order that is a memorandum order until its price is reached or passed is a stop order. ______

14. Interest on corporate bonds is based on a 365-day year. ______

15. On a sell trade, commission is added to the trade monies to arrive at the net the client is to receive. ______

16. Transactions usually occur between two principals who do not know each other. ______

17. Pending orders are organized in a strict time sequence. ______

18. The types of securities the public is interested in is determined by the order room. ______

19. Every trade that a brokerage firm processes must undergo a series of computations. ______

20. Part of the booking procedure is the recording of fees and commissions due to the firm. ______

21. A discrepancy in trade information appears on the compared listing. ______

22. After orders are properly coded, dated, and calculated, they are sent to the order room. ______

23. When a transaction involves bonds, interest has to be accrued and paid by the buyer to the seller. ______

24. A spread order is used in listed options and futures trading. ______

25. A market order is an order to execute at whatever the market price is when the broker enters the crowd. ______

Answer Sheet

Matching Quiz

13 limit order
8 comparison
16 FOK
14 market order
2 confirmation
17 AON
6 stop
15 figuration
12 product mix
5 code
11 blotter
7 clearing corporation
4 booking
10 contract sheet
3 CUSIP

Multiple Choice

1. a
2. b
3. a
4. e
5. b
6. d
7. a
8. e
9. b
10. c
11. c

True/False

12. F
13. T
14. F
15. F
16. T
17. F
18. F
19. T
20. T
21. F
22. F
23. T
24. T
25. T

Note: Total of points is 103.

LESSON FOUR

The Margin and Cashiering Departments

READING ASSIGNMENT

Chapter 8 Margin
Chapter 9 Cashiering

OBJECTIVES

- To understand the roles of the *margin* and *cashiering departments*.
- To properly position the functions of the *margin* and *cashiering departments* in relation to the overall operations.
- To define *loan value, debit balance, equity,* and *margin rate*.

READING ORIENTATION

The material covered in Chapters 8 and 9 of the text describe the functions of the next two departments of the operations procedure.

The *margin department* monitors the current status of each customer's account. This is where the majority of a customer/firm rules are enforced. This department also determines which customers may or may not purchase securities on margin.

The *cashiering department* is responsible for moving all securities and funds within the firm. Other tasks include receiving and delivering, vaulting, and security transfers.

KEY TERMS

Bearer form, 89
Broker's call rate, 91
Buying power, 78
Collateral loan, 91
Credit balance, 76
Current market value, 76
Debit balance, 74, 76
Dirty stock, 89
Equity, 74, 76
Finder, 92
Free stock, 91
Loan value, 73, 77
Maintenance call, 80
Marginable, 73
Margin purchase, 72–73
Margin rate, 74, 75
Money manager, 91
Regulation T, 75
Reorganization, 93
Repurchase agreement, 92
Restricted account, 81
Seg securities, 91
Special miscellaneous account, 81
Transfer agent, 92–93
Uncollateralized loan, 91

Challenge

MATCHING QUIZ

Match each term at the left with a definition at the right, by placing the number of the definition in the fill-in space next to the term. There are more definitions than terms. (Each question is worth 2 points.)

_____ **equity**

_____ **regulation T**

_____ **seg securities**

_____ **loan value**

_____ **buying power**

_____ **margin rate**

_____ **SMA**

_____ **finder**

_____ **money manager**

_____ **bearer instrument**

_____ **debit balance**

_____ **vaulting**

_____ **repos**

1. Locates loanable securities for a fee.

2. Maintains the company's list of owners.

3. Amount that can be lent.

4. Portion of account's value belonging to the customer.

5. Securing customers' securities.

6. Special miscellaneous account for bookkeeping purposes.

7. Securities unavailable for loan.

8. Responsible for all of the firm's financing.

9. When a brokerage firm sells securities to the financing organization with the agreement that the firm will repurchase them in the near future.

10. Keeps track of changes among issuers and makes appropriate changes in customer accounts.

11. Amount that has been loaned.

12. Minimum deposit required by a customer.

13. Backbone of all margin rules.

14. Unregistered instrument.

15. The dollar amount worth of securities that can be purchased without depositing additional funds.

MULTIPLE CHOICE

Select the letter that best answers the numbered question. (Each question is worth 5 points.)

1. The responsibility for maintaining customer accounts in accordance with the various rules and regulations belongs to the:

a) P&S department
b) transfer department
c) margin department
d) dividend department
e) stock record department

2. The difference between *loan value* and *debit balance* is:

a) loan value is the amount that can be borrowed, debit balance is the amount that has been borrowed
b) loan value is the amount that has been borrowed for the client, debit balance is the amount the firm owes
c) loan value represents the client's funds, debit balance represents funds the client borrowed
d) loan value and debit balance have the same meaning

3. If the margin rate is 50 percent, and the client has $5,000 excess, what is the buying power?

a) 2,500
b) 5,000
c) 7,500
d) 10,000
e) insufficient information given

4. The department responsible for the movement of securities and funds involved with operations is the:

a) P&S department
b) margin department
c) cashiers department
d) stock record department
e) accounts receivable department

5. The process by which firms pledge security at banks to support debit balances in margin accounts is known as:

- **a)** stock loan
- **b)** hypothecation
- **c)** legal transfer
- **d)** reorganization
- **e)** going public

6. The usual minimum interest rate charged by banks for collateral loans is known as:

- **a)** margin rate
- **b)** broker's call rate
- **c)** buying power
- **d)** equity
- **3)** current market value

7. What is *money due on T calls*?

- **a)** the equity owed by a customer on a transaction
- **b)** the sum owed by a firm on a transaction
- **c)** clearance of a check
- **d)** the sum owed to the firm on a transaction
- **e)** receiving and delivering of securities

8. What is one of the main functions of the cashiering department?

- **a)** borrowing and lending money
- **b)** vaulting
- **c)** receiving
- **d)** delivering
- **e)** all of the above

Questions 9 and 10 refer to the following scenario:

Customer Bill Purchases 200 shares of XYZ at 60 for a total cost of $12,000. With the margin rate of 50 percent, the brokerage firm receives Bill's check for $6,000 and lends the rest to the customer. The equity is then $6,000.

9. If XYZ falls in value to 20, what would the equity be?

a) $6,000

b) $4,000

c) −$2,000 (deficit)

d) $2,000

10. Firms send *calls* to customers for additional money when:

a) the equity goes below one-third the debit balance

b) the equity goes below one-half the debit balance

c) the debit balance goes below one-third the equity

d) the equity decreases to zero

TRUE/FALSE

Questions 11-22 are either true or false. Mark T for true, F for false. (Each question is worth 2 points.)

11. When a margin account's loan value is greater than the debit balance, the account has excess. ______

12. The sum of money owed by a customer on a transaction is known as a maintenance call. ______

13. Securities that a brokerage firm pledges at a bank to secure funds for margin accounts are known as hypothecated securities. ______

14. Debit balance is the amount of money loaned by the firm or owed by the customer. ______

15. How much the firm can lend the customer is determined by the debit balance. ______

16. Securities are marginable when the firm can borrow money on them. ______

17. Equity = Current market value − Debit balance. ______

18. Banks charge lower rates of interest for collateral loans. ______

19. Dirty stock is a security that is in good deliverable form. ______

20. The work of the margin department is the last checkpoint before the customer gets involved. ______

21. If a customer fails to pay for a purchased security, the security is activated. ______

22. A restricted account has a debit balance that is higher than the current loan value. ______

Answer Sheet

Matching Quiz

4 equity
13 regulation T
7 seg securities
3 loan value
15 buying power
12 margin rate
6 SMA
1 finder
8 money manager
14 bearer instrument
11 debit balance
5 vaulting
9 repos

Multiple Choice

1. c
2. a
3. d
4. c
5. b
6. b
7. d
8. e
9. c
10. a

True/False

11. T
12. F
13. T
14. T
15. F
16. T
17. T
18. T
19. F
20. T
21. F
22. T

LESSON FIVE

Accounting-Oriented Tasks

READING ASSIGNMENT

Chapter 10 Stock Record
Chapter 11 Accounting: The Daily Cash Record
Chapter 12 Dividend

OBJECTIVES

- To understand the importance of the stock record.
- To identify the components of the accounting department.
- To describe the dividend cycle.

READING ORIENTATION

Chapters 10 through 12 discuss accounting-oriented tasks in the overall operations function.

The *stock record,* which is a department, as well as a document, provides one of the firm's most valuable records. This ledger reports on all security movements and positions every day.

The *accounting department* provides another important document known as the *daily cash record.* Produced each business day, this listing contains all the money movements that occurred in the firm on the previous business day.

The *dividend department* has the task of figuring and properly crediting dividends to individual's accounts. This function ties all accounts affected by dividend payments to the actual sum received from the paying agent.

KEY TERMS

Accounting journal, 102
Accruals, 102
Adjusted trial balance, 102–103
Assets, 103
Audit, 97–98
Balance sheet, 103
Break, 96
Corporate registrar, 111
Daily cash record, 99, 102
Declaration date, 107
DDA, 111
Dividend, 107
Dividend cycle, 107–109
DNR, 109
Due bill, 113
Earnings report, 103
Ex-dividend date, 109
Income statement, 103
Liability, 103
Net worth, 103
Payable date, 107
Profit and loss statement, 103
Record date, 107
Reverse split, 110
Stock dividend, 109–110
Stock record, 94
Stock split, 110
Street-side position, 111
Transfer agent, 111
Trial balance, 102

Challenge

MATCHING QUIZ

Match each term at the left with a definition at the right, by placing the number of the definition in the fill-in space next to the term. There are more definitions than terms. (Each question is worth 1 point.)

_____ **street-side positions**

_____ **stock dividend**

_____ **P&L statement**

_____ **liability**

_____ **stock split**

_____ **income**

_____ **expense**

_____ **asset**

_____ **record date**

_____ **break**

_____ **declaration date**

_____ **accrual**

_____ **due bill**

_____ **ex-dividend date**

_____ **daily cash report**

1. An IOU.

2. Accounts reflecting security locations.

3. When a dividend is paid.

4. Holders receive one or more shares of additional issue for each share held.

5. Inventory.

6. Money movements that occurred in the firm on the previous business day.

7. Commission.

8. Reports on revenue earned and expenses incurred over a period.

9. When only one side of an entry is recorded.

10. Shareholder's equity.

11. Price is adjusted by the amount of the dividend.

12. Paid as a percentage of outstanding stock.

13. Dividend is announced.

14. To whom dividend is paid.

15. Salaries payable.

16. Rent.

17. Payable at another time.

MULTIPLE CHOICE

Select the letter that best answers the numbered question. (Each question is worth 5 points.)

1. Recording and balancing of all security movements within the firm is the responsibility of the:

a) P&S department

b) margin department

c) cashiers department

d) stock record department

e) dividend department

2. The three component parts of a *balance sheet* are:

a) income, expense, net worth

b) assets, income, expense

c) assets, liability, net worth

d) liability, income, expense

e) net worth, retained earnings, sales

3. Dividends and bond interest payments will be made to whoever is the *registered holder*. To be eligible to receive the payment directly from the issuer, the security must be in your name on the:

a) record date

b) payable date

c) ex-dividend date

d) declaration date

e) proxy date

4. *TUV security* is recorded as having been removed from the vault, but the record does not show when it was delivered. This is an example of:

a) daily cash record

b) trial balance

c) declaration date

d) audit

e) break

5. The final step in the accounting process is:

a) purchase and sales

b) margin account

c) daily cash record

d) trial balance

e) audit

6. For cash dividends, the ex-dividend date is:

a) four business days before the record date

b) two business days before the record date

c) four business days after the record date

d) T + 4

3) the payable date

7. The balance sheet is set up so that the total of assets equals:

a) the difference between the liabilities and net worth

b) the sum of total liabilities and net worth

c) the sum of the income and expenses

d) all the expenses

e) none of the above

8. What is accomplished by a trial balance?

a) All accounts with debit balances should equal all the accounts with credit balances

b) All entries have been posted from the daily journals to the ledger

c) The balance in each account is updated and carried forward

d) All of the above

e) None of the above

9. When a security is received from a customer, the customer's account is debited and the firm's box (vault) account is:

a) audited

b) balanced

c) moved

d) credited

d) adjusted

10. When a firm acts as a custodian for its customer's securities, what must be credited to each such account?

- **a)** commissions
- **b)** dividends
- **c)** taxes
- **d)** interest charges
- **e)** net worth

11. The dividend cycle consists of what three important dates?

- **a)** declaration, dividend, payable
- **b)** payable, record, transfer
- **c)** declaration, record, payable
- **d)** record, declaration, trade
- **e)** settlement, dividend, record

12. In a profit and loss statement, credit accounts exceed debit accounts, the brokerage firm has:

- **a)** incurred a loss
- **b)** broken even
- **c)** gone out of business
- **d)** failed to pay taxes
- **e)** made a profit

TRUE/FALSE

Questions 13–26 are either true or false. Mark T for true, F for false. (Each question is worth 2 points.)

13. The balance sheet is an accounting report that shows income and expenses incurred during a period. ______

14. In dividend situations, the ex-dividend date is the first day that a purchaser of the stock is not entitled to receive the dividend. ______

15. Stock splits represent a distribution of earnings by the issuing corporation. ______

16. The daily cash record serves as an accounting journal. ______

17. Account numbers denote branches, among other things. ______

18. To properly record the movement of securities, the stock record must balance debits versus assets. ______

19. In an audit, all certificates are counted or verified in writing and compared to the stock record. ______

20. The actual payment of dividends is made by the transfer agent. ______

21. For listed stocks, the ex-dividend date is four business days before the record date. ______

22. Balance sheets contain all the debits and credits in the adjusted trial balance. ______

23. The profit and loss statement reports all revenue earned and all expenses incurred by the firm. ______

24. All accounts in the adjusted trial balance are used to develop the P&L statement and the audit sheet. ______

25. A trial balance is performed in the dividend department. ______

26. The stock record must be in balance at all times. ______

Answer Sheet

Matching Quiz

2 street-side positions
12 stock dividend
8 P & L statement
15 liability
4 stock split
7 income
16 expense
5 asset
14 record date
9 break
13 declaration date
17 accrual
1 due bill
11 ex-dividend date
6 daily cash report

Multiple Choice

1. d
2. c
3. a
4. e
5. d
6. a
7. b
8. d
9. d
10. b
11. c
12. e

True/False

13. F
14. T
15. F
16. T
17. T
18. F
19. T
20. F
21. T
22. F
23. T
24. F
25. F
26. T

LESSON SIX

Proxy Procedure, New Account Procedures and Compliance

READING ASSIGNMENT

Chapter 13 Proxy
Chapter 14 New Accounts
Chapter 15 Compliance

OBJECTIVES

- To understand the reason for enabling a proxy vote.
- To identify the basic types of accounts a customer can have.
- To list the identifying information needed for an account.
- To realize the importance of compliance with the rules and regulations of the securities industry.

READING ORIENTATION

The three chapters covered in this lesson briefly discuss the *proxy procedure,* the information needed for a *new account,* and *compliance*.

Brokerage firms deal with numbers, names, IDs, and more numbers every second of every day. In order to keep this information in workable order, it must be accurate and complete. The *new accounts department* ensures that all the necessary information on a customer is obtained and all the required forms are on file.

The rules and regulations of the securities industry could fill several texts, and in fact do, which is why compliance with these rules is only briefly touched upon in this book.

KEY TERMS

Corporate resolution, 122
Fiduciary account, 128
Full power of attorney, 122
Individual cash account, 118
Joint account, 121
Lending agreement, 121
Limited power of attorney, 122
Margin agreement, 121
Margin account, 120–121
Master file, 120
New account form, 118–120
Power of attorney account, 122
Proxy fight, 117
Proxy statement, 115
Registered representative, 126
Signature card, 120

Challenge

MATCHING QUIZ

Match each term at the left with a definition at the right, by placing the number of the definition in the fill-in space next to the term. There are more definitions than terms. (Each question is worth 4 points.)

_____ **procedures**

_____ **corporate resolution**

_____ **proxy**

_____ **margin agreement**

_____ **tenants in common**

_____ **limited power of attorney**

_____ **margin account**

_____ **lending agreement**

_____ **master file**

_____ **proxy fight**

1. Sets forth the terms under which the firm will lend money to the customer.

2. Permits the designated holder to enter buy and sell orders only.

3. A new account form.

4. Daily, weekly, monthly, and quarterly routines.

5. An agreement whereby the death of one principal has no effect on the survivor's percentage of ownership in an account.

6. Permanent record of the customer's signature.

7. Lists all current accounts by number, name, address.

8. Authorizes one or more of the company's officers to transact business in the corporation's name and for its benefit.

9. The customer borrows money from the brokerage firm to buy securities.

10. Enables the shareholder to vote for members of management and other key issues affecting the corporation.

11. A firm lends a margined security to other firms or against other customers' short sales.

12. Two groups vie for control of the corporation.

MULTIPLE CHOICE

Select the letter that best answers the numbered question. (Each question is worth 3 points.)

1. Stock maintained by the firm in its name for the benefit of the customer is said to be:

a) in the name of the beneficial owner
b) in a nominee name
c) non-negotiable
d) improperly registered
e) owned by the firm

2. Customers whose stock is registered in the firm's name,

a) lose their right to vote
b) will be notified how the firm voted the stock
c) will vote by proxies sent to them by the firm
d) may receive a pass from the firm to attend corporate meetings
e) may vote only if the stock pays a dividend

3. Margin accounts require which of the following sets of papers?

I. new accounts form
II. margin agreement
III. trust agreement
IV. loan agreement
V. custody agreement

a) I and IV
b) I, II and IV
c) II, III and IV
d) I, IV and V
e) II, IV and V

4. A proxy fight occurs when:

a) four groups vie for control of a corporation

b) two groups vie for control of a corporation

c) two groups vie for control of a trade

d) a vote is lost in the mail

e) members of management disagree

5. In a cash account, all securities must be paid in full by the ______ business day, but no later than the ______.

a) 2nd/5th

b) 4th/5th

c) 5th/8th

d) 5th/7th

e) 3rd/6th

6. A joint account is an account in which two individuals may:

a) conduct transactions

b) be established as husband and wife

c) buy each other out

d) pay interest

e) borrow money

7. The "know your customer" rule requires brokers to have their customers' goals in writing. What would this include?

a) growth

b) income

c) speculation

d) all of the above

e) none of the above

8. What routine ensures that the accounts are in proper order?

a) daily routine

b) compliance

c) lending agreement

d) weekly routine

e) quarterly routine

9. A new client is ready to enter an order when:

a) a margin agreement is signed

b) an account is properly opened

c) a signature card is signed

d) a salesman takes his/her name down

e) a proxy statement is signed

TRUE/FALSE

Questions 10–20 are either true or false. Mark T for true, F for false. (Each question is worth 3 points.)

10. In establishing a customer account, a limited power of attorney permits the holder of such a power to withdraw and deposit funds and securities. ______

11. A client must sign a lending agreement when opening a cash account. ______

12. The responsibility of informing clients of corporate meetings and so on, concerning securities owned by the client but maintained in the firm's name belongs to the proxy department. ______

13. Compliance is restricted to one department. ______

14. Another name for a stockbroker is a registered representative. ______

15. Customers trading options or future contracts have to sign a form stating that they understand the risks and/or conditions of such transactions. ______

16. In a joint tenant with rights of survivorship account, if one principal dies, the entire account becomes void. ______

17. It is the responsibility of the proxy department to properly document all the firm's customer accounts. ______

18. Failure to provide your social security number to your broker will result in dividends and interest being withheld at a rate of 30 percent. ______

19. The compliance department employees make certain that brokers are correctly registered for the type of business they are conducting. ______

20. With a corporate account, the brokerage firm must obtain a copy of the corporate charter. ______

Answer Sheet

Matching Quiz

4 procedures
8 corporate resolution
10 proxy
1 margin agreement
5 tenants in common
2 limited power of attorney
9 margin account
11 lending agreement
7 master file
12 proxy fight

Multiple Choice

1. b
2. c
3. b
4. b
5. d
6. a
7. d
8. e
9. b

True/False

10. F
11. F
12. T
13. F
14. T
15. T
16. F
17. F
18. F
19. T
20. T

LESSON SEVEN

Electronic Date Processing and the Role of Banks

READING ASSIGNMENT

Chapter 16 Electronic Date Processing (EDP)
Chapter 17 The Role of Banks

OBJECTIVES

- To understand the different types of computer systems.
- To know the responsibilities of the data processing manager.
- To be able to identify the various roles of commercial banks.

READING ORIENTATION

Chapter 16 discusses the importance of *electronic data processing* in a brokerage firm. The computer center supervises the transmitting network. By day and night, it processes data, calculates, and generates reports.

Chapter 17 briefly talks about several important roles a *commercial bank* plays in the brokerage industry. For instance, it makes short-term credit available, extends loans to brokerage firms, and facilitates international trade.

KEY TERMS

Commercial paper, 147
Computer language, 134
Computer system, 133
Data, 133–134
Debug, 140–141
Discount form, 147
Executive program, 133
Fed fund, 148
Hardware, 133
In-house, 131
Investment banker, 145
Locked up in seg, 145
Mainframe, 135–136
Member bank, 148
Message-switch program, 135–136
Microcomputer, 137
Minicomputer, 136–137
Minimum margin requirement, 144
Overnight, 143
Pending tape, 139
Plus interest, 147
Prime rate, 146
Processing program, 133
Programmer, 134
Routine, 134
Sales credit, 139
Segregated, 144
Service bureau, 138
Settled position, 143
Settlement date position, 143
Software, 133
Subroutine, 134
Trading position, 143

Challenge

MATCHING QUIZ

Match each term at the left with a definition at the right, by placing the number of the definition in the fill-in space next to the term. There are more definitions than terms. (Each question is worth 2½ points.)

_____ **Fed funds**

_____ **message-switch program**

_____ **routine**

_____ **in-house**

_____ **locked up in seg**

_____ **service bureau**

_____ **trading position**

_____ **investment banker**

_____ **prime rate**

_____ **same-day settler**

_____ **clearing-house funds**

_____ **microcomputer**

1. EDP equipment is on the firm's premises and used exclusively by the firm.

2. Brokerage firm.

3. Trades settled on the same day as execution.

4. Securities that traders have positioned for the purpose of trading.

5. Same-day money.

6. Securities cannot be used by the firm for loan purposes.

7. The corresponding output must be in the hands of users first thing in the morning.

8. Used to compute yields and yield equivalents between issues.

9. Enables the mainframe to route messages, orders, and reports from point A to point B.

10. A company that specializes in computer processing.

11. Rate at which banks will lend money to their financially strongest clients.

12. Checks clear in much the same manner as a personal checking account.

13. Agency commissions and the markups on principal transactions.

14. Brings the computer to an unwanted halt.

15. Programs run in interconnected cycles.

MULTIPLE CHOICE

Select the letter that best answers the numbered question. (Each question is worth 3½ points.)

1. The *data processing manager's responsibilities* encompass the following three areas:

a) microcomputers, minicomputers, mainframes

b) production, programming, forward planning

c) production, figuration, bankers acceptances

d) cash flow summary, programming, corporate issues

e) forward planning, production, loans

2. *Settled positions* include which of the following?

a) Securities bought and paid for, but not in good deliverable form or not sold

b) Physical inventory owned

c) Securities sold but not delivered

d) All of the above

e) None of the above

3. What does *fed funds* mean?

a) federal money

b) wired money

c) clearing-house money

d) discounted money

e) same-day money

4. Firms must over-collateralize *margin loans* by what percent?

a) 40

b) 50

c) 25

d) 60

e) 75

5. The *hardware* and *software* combine to make up the:

- **a)** program
- **b)** bug
- **c)** computer system
- **d)** EDP department
- **e)** routine

6. Which computer is commonly used in the sales area because of its speed and ease of use?

- **a)** mainframe
- **b)** minicomputer
- **c)** routine
- **d)** microcomputer
- **e)** CRT terminal

7. On *commercial loans,* banks charge a rate of interest based on:

- **a)** the minimum margin requirement
- **b)** the prime lending rate
- **c)** the Reg-T requirement
- **d)** the dividend value
- **e)** the cash value of the security

8. The *logical set of instructions* for the computer is called the:

- **a)** hardware
- **b)** mainframe
- **c)** memory
- **d)** software
- **e)** service bureau

9. In settling *government trades,* which department of the brokerage firm instructs the agent what to receive and what to deliver each day?

- **a)** EDP department
- **b)** clearing house
- **c)** cashier's department
- **d)** margin department
- **e)** stock record department

10. *Loans* that can be collateralized or uncollateralized are:

a) municipal bonds
b) commercial loans
c) margin loans
d) plus interest loans
e) brokerage loans

TRUE/FALSE

Questions 11–20 are either true or false. Mark T for true, F for false. (Each question is worth 3½ points.)

11. To satisfy corporate clients' needs, banks issue short-term debt instruments (on behalf of the corporation), known as commercial paper. ______

12. Firms that deal in government securities turn to other firms for their cashiering function. ______

13. Programs are continuously written, tested, debugged, and tested again whenever there are problems. ______

14. The processing programs need codes to produce their output. ______

15. Trading positions, settlement date positions, and settled positions are types of inventory positions. ______

16. One of Regulation T's requirements is that a firm may use up to 140 percent of a margin account's debit balance to secure financing. ______

17. Commercial paper is traded as a bond. ______

18. Banks buy and sell securities from inventory positions that they maintain for trusts and other institutions. ______

19. Securities in customers' long and short positions are in a settled position. ______

20. Municipal bonds are brought to market through competitive underwriting. ______

Answer Sheet

Matching Quiz

5 fed funds
9 message-switch program
15 routine
1 in-house
6 locked up in seg
10 service bureau
4 trading position
2 investment banker
11 prime rate
3 same-day settler
12 clearing-house funds
8 microcomputer

Multiple Choice

1. b
2. d
3. e
4. a
5. c
6. d
7. b
8. d
9. c
10. b

True/False

11. T
12. F
13. T
14. T
15. T
16. T
17. F
18. T
19. T
20. T

LESSON EIGHT

Corporate Securities: Common Stocks and Preferred Stocks

READING ASSIGNMENT

Chapter 18 Corporate Securities
Chapter 19 Common Stock
Chapter 20 Preferred Stocks

OBJECTIVES

- To understand the difference between common stock and preferred stock.
- To be able to describe how common stock is traded.
- To discuss the underwriting procedure of a preferred stock.

READING ORIENTATION

This lesson familiarizes the student with basic information regarding *corporate securities*—their differences and general characteristics.

Chapter 19 briefly describes *common stock,* which represents ownership in a corporation. Underwriting and trading procedures are also discussed.

Chapter 20 talks about *preferred stock,* which is similar to common stock. The difference between the two is that preferred stocks pay dividends to their owner. Other differences such as those in procedures and requirements are also discussed.

KEY TERMS

Above parity, 166
Arbitrageur, 166
Auction market, 159
Bond, 153
Callable, 165
Cash dividend, 158
Common stock, 153, 155
Conversion rate, 165
Convertible, 165
Corporate registrar, 160
Cumulative preferred, 167–168
Dealer, 159
Dividend disbursing agent, 160
Dollar rate, 161
Fixed-income securities, 164
Investment banker, 158
Limited liability, 153
Listed security, 159
Make a market, 159
Mark-up, 159
Negotiate, 158–159
Nominee registration, 159
Noncallable, 165
Noncumulative preferred, 167–168
Odd lot, 159
Parity, 165–166
Participating preferred, 168
Percentage, 164
Preferred stock, 161
Privately owned, 158
Public offering, 158
Registered issue, 159
Round lot, 159
Shareholder, 153
State of incorporation, 153
Stock dividend, 158
Street name, 159
Transfer agent, 160
Underwriting, 158

Challenge

MATCHING QUIZ

Match each term at the left with a definition at the right, by placing the number of the definition in the fill-in space next to the term. There are more definitions than terms. (Each question is worth 1 point.)

______ **cumulative preferred**

______ **par value**

______ **callable**

______ **conversion rate**

______ **participating preferred**

______ **auction market**

______ **8%/$50 par value preferred**

______ **stock dividend**

______ **parity**

______ **abitrageur**

______ **cash dividend**

______ **round lot**

______ **shareholder**

______ **limited liability**

1. The number of shares that can be had for each share of preferred.

2. Pays interest only when earned.

3. Pays $4.00 per share, per year.

4. Paid on a per-share basis.

5. Dividends that are not paid, then accumulate.

6. Buys preferred stock, converts it, then sells the common stock.

7. An investor who buys the corporation's stock.

8. Permits the corporation to retire an issue at its option for a predetermined price.

9. Paid as a percentage of shares owned.

10. Shares in dividends with common at prearranged terms.

11. Amount of sales charge.

12. When the market price of a preferred stock is equal to that of the converted number of common stock.

13. Unit of trading of 100 shares.

14. Shareholders are liable only for the total amounts of their investment.

15. Value assigned to a stock for bookkeeping purposes.

16. Highest bid and lowest offer have priority.

MULTIPLE CHOICE

Select the letter that best answers the numbered question. (Each question is worth 4 points.)

1. Ownership in a corporation is represented by:

I. common stock
II. rights
III. preferred stock
IV. bonds
V. notes

a) I only
b) IV and V
c) I and II
d) I and III
e) I, II and III

Questions 2-4 are based on the following:

Assume the ZAP Company has one share of *common stock* and one share of $8 *preferred stock*. Assume also that the company pays 100 percent of its earnings out in dividends. Using the following chart, compute the total dividend earned by the preferred shareholder under the stated conditions.

Year	1	2	3	4	5	Total
Earning	$14	$6	$26	$4	$5	$55

2. If the $8 preferred was a *straight preferred* (non-cumulative, nonparticipating), what is the total dividend earned by the shareholder for the five-year period?

a) $16
b) $40
c) $31
d) 0
e) $15

3. If the $8 preferred was a *cumulative* (nonparticipating) *preferred,* the dividends earned for the five years would be:

a) $40
b) $33
c) $30
d) 0
e) $45

4. Assume the $8 *preferred* is a participating preferred that states that the common shareholder can receive up to $8 in dividends per year after which the one share of *preferred* and one share of *common* will share equally in the remainder. What would be the preferred shareholder's total dividend for the five-year period?

a) $36
b) $40
c) $33
d) $41
e) 0

5. WIP common stock is trading at $30 per share; the corporate bone $1,000 WIP 8% FA—2006 is convertible into 25 shares of common stock. What would the *bond* be selling at if it were at parity?

a) $1,000
b) $800
c) $750
d) $500
e) $1,200

6. A *stock* that gives the holder the right to exchange it for shares of common stock of the same company is called:

a) listed security
b) callable
c) convertible
d) cumulative
e) preferred

7. *New issues* are brought to public market through:

- **a)** negotiation
- **b)** auction
- **c)** barter
- **d)** underwriting
- **e)** word of mouth

8. A 10 percent stock dividend means that for every 100 shares you own, you receive how many additional shares?

- **a)** 10
- **b)** 20
- **c)** 30
- **d)** 50
- **e)** 0

9. If a *common stock* is registered in the name of the firm or a bank (in behalf of the owner), then it is registered in:

- **a)** the beneficial owner's behalf
- **b)** the OTC market
- **c)** the customer's name
- **d)** street name
- **e)** round lots

10. Which of the following can be considered *fixed income securities*?

I. preferred stock
II. corporate bond
III. municipal bond
IV. U.S. government obligations
V. common stock

- **a)** I and V
- **b)** I, II and III
- **c)** II and IV
- **d)** II, III and V
- **e)** I, II, II and IV

11. If a corporation and its investment banker believe that the price of the company's common stock is likely to *rise* over time, what may they offer?

a) a callable issue

b) a convertible preferred

c) a cumulative preferred

d) a cash dividend

e) a participating preferred

12. To keep track of ownership, an issuing entity retains the services of *one registrar,* one or two *transfer agents,* and:

a) two shareholders

b) one dealer

c) arbitrageur

d) one dividend disbursing agent

e) one negotiator

TRUE/FALSE

Questions 13–26 are either true or false. Mark T for true, F for false. (Each question is worth 2 points.)

13. Par value of a stock is the same as the market value. ______

14. All shareholders are owners and therefore have the right to vote. ______

15. A round lot for trading in common stock is 100 shares. ______

16. Securities that can be retired on demand by the issuer is known as convertible securities. ______

17. A dealer is a person who buys and sells securities for his own trading account. ______

18. Common stock is a registered issue. ______

19. The market price of preferred stock is based on current yield rates for fixed income investments. ______

20. If a preferred stock is worth less than the value of the converted common stock, it is said to be above parity. ______

21. Preferred stock pays a variable rate of dividend. ______

22. A dealer makes a profit by adding a mark-up to the securities it buys and sells. ______

23. In preferred stocks, dividend percentage is a percentage of the selling price. ______

24. Cash dividends are usually paid annually, semiannually or quarterly. ______

Answer Sheet

Matching Quiz

5 cumulative preferred
15 par value
8 callable
1 conversion rate
10 participating preferred
16 auction market
3 eight percent/$50 par value preferred
9 stock dividend
12 parity
6 arbitrageur
4 cash dividend
13 round lot
7 shareholder
14 limited liability

Multiple Choice

1. e
2. c
3. b
4. a
5. c
6. c
7. d
8. a
9. d
10. e
11. b
12. d

True/False

13. F
14. F
15. T
16. F
17. T
18. T
19. T
20. F
21. F
22. F
23. F
24. T

LESSON NINE

Corporate Bonds, Notes, Rights, and Warrants

READING ASSIGNMENT

Chapter 21 Corporate Bonds and Notes
Chapter 22 Rights and Warrants

OBJECTIVES

- To distinguish the difference between bonds and notes.
- To list the different types of bonds.
- To understand how interest is computed on a bond.
- To define rights and warrants.

READING ORIENTATION

Corporate bondholders and *noteholders* are creditors, or lenders, to the corporation. Bonds are long-term, and notes are intermediate-term debt instruments. Chapter 21 discusses bonds and notes: their differences and similarities.

Rights and warrants are other means for a company to raise additional capital. They both permit holders to subscribe to new shares, but for different lengths of time. They are discussed in Chapter 22.

KEY TERMS

Arbitrageur, 184–185
At a discount, 173
At a premium, 173
Bearer certificate, 180
Below par, 173
Bond, 169, 172
Certificate, 189
Closed-end, 179
Collateral trust bond, 179
Commercial loan, 169
Conversion, 178
Coupon rate, 174
Cum rights, 185
Debenture bond, 179
Equipment trust bond, 179
Fully-registered bond, 180
Income bond, 181
Indenture, 178
Leverage, 172
Liquidate, 180
Mortgage bond, 179
Note, 169
Open-ended, 179
Over par, 173
Par, 173
Preemptive rights, 184
Receiver's certificate, 180
Redemption, 178
Refunding, 178
Registered to principal, 180
Right, 182–184
Sinking fund, 178
Subscription, 182
Theoretical value, 184
Unit, 186
Warrant, 186
Yield, 174

Challenge

MATCHING QUIZ

Match each term at the left with a definition at the right, by placing the number of the definition in the fill-in space next to the term. There are more definitions than terms. (Each question is worth 2½ points.)

_____ **indenture**

_____ **sinking fund**

_____ **rights**

_____ **debenture**

_____ **income bond**

_____ **yield**

_____ **leverage**

_____ **theoretical value**

_____ **mortgage bond**

_____ **warrant**

_____ **refunding**

_____ **coupon rate**

1. Earnings set aside to pay off a bond issue.

2. Bond backed by the company's good name.

3. Bonds backed by real estate of the issuer.

4. Investment in short-term instruments.

5. Terms of the debt.

6. Rate of return.

7. The corporation retires one bond issue by issuing another.

8. The difference between the subscription price and the market price divided by the number of rights required to purchase one new share.

9. The stated interest on the bond.

10. A security that gives stockholders the opportunity to purchase additional shares in proportion to their present holdings.

11. Entitles the holder to convert the security into common stock at a set price, during a set time.

12. Pays interest only when earned.

13. Pays dividends not interest.

14. Using borrowed money to make money.

MULTIPLE CHOICE

Select the letter that best answers the numbered question. (Each question is worth 4 points.)

1. Corporate bonds secured by real estate are known as:

a) real estate bonds
b) mortgage bonds
c) collateral trust bonds
d) equipment trust bonds
e) debenture bonds

2. JEB Corp. has 5,000,000 shares of common stock outstanding. It wants to issue 1,000,000 more shares through a rights offering. To ensure that the terms of preemptive rights are satisfied, how many rights must JEB Corp. issue?

a) 1,000,000
b) 5,000,000
c) 6,000,000
d) 1 for each 100 shares
e) insufficient information given

3. RAP & RAP Inc. common stock is trading at 75 cum-rights. The company has announced a rights offering to subscribe to new shares at a rate of four rights plus $70 for each new share. What is the value of a right?

a) $1.00
b) $1.25
c) $5.00
d) $4.00
e) $0.25

4. Which of the following entitles a holder to convert a security into common stock at a set price during a specified period of time?

- **a)** unit
- **b)** right
- **c)** warrant
- **d)** bond
- **e)** convertible preferred

5. The quoted price of a bond represents a percentage of the:

- **a)** interest
- **b)** dividends
- **c)** refund
- **d)** principal
- **e)** face value

6. Payment of interest on a bond is made on the same day of the month throughout the life of the instrument. Which notation best illustrates this?

- **a)** F&A 15
- **b)** F&J 15
- **c)** A&N 10
- **d)** M&J
- **e)** J&A 23

7. What has the most influence on income-bearing or fixed dividend securities?

- **a)** bond prices
- **b)** interest rate fluctuations
- **c)** dividends
- **d)** coupon rates
- **e)** length of ownership

8. What may be retired by redemption, conversion, or refunding?

a) stocks
b) notes
c) warrants
d) certificates
e) bonds

9. In a warrant, the value of each issue is determined by the following:

I. the conversion price
II. time remaining in the warrant
III. value of the issue's underlying stock
IV. the prime rate
V. the market price

a) I and IV
b) I, II and V
c) III and V
d) II, III and IV
e) I, II and III

10. Corporate bonds and notes are brought to the public market through:

a) auctions
b) underwritings
c) warrants
d) word of mouth
e) advertisement

TRUE/FALSE

Questions 11–22 are either true or false. Mark T for true, F for false. (Each question is worth 2½ points.)

11. A $1,000 bond trading at "96" will cost $96 plus accrued interest. ______

12. The terms and conditions affecting a corporate debt, as evidenced by and printed on a bond, is known as indenture. ______

13. The process by which bonds are retired through the issuance of new debt instruments is known as refunding. ______

14. Rights become worthless if not exercised or sold by the date stated in the certificate. ______

15. A bond certificate is evidence of the debt owed the bondholder by the issuing corporation. ______

16. Corporate bonds are obligations issued by a state agency. ______

17. Bondholders receive interest; stockholders receive dividends. ______

18. An open-ended mortgage issue is one where subsequent issues are equal in all respects to the original issue. ______

19. Warrants are shorter-term issues than rights. ______

20. Warrant holders are generally entitled to a purchase price that is higher than the stock's current market price. ______

21. For a fully-registered bond, the name of the owner is maintained by a corporate registrar. ______

22. Income bonds have an extremely low interest rate. ______

Answer Sheet

Matching Quiz

5 indenture
1 sinking fund
10 rights
2 debenture
12 income bond
6 yield
14 leverage
8 theoretical value
3 mortgage bond
11 warrant
7 refunding
9 coupon rate

Multiple Choice

1. b
2. b
3. a
4. c
5. d
6. a
7. b
8. e
9. e
10. b

True/False

11. F
12. T
13. T
14. T
15. T
16. F
17. T
18. T
19. F
20. T
21. T
22. F

LESSON TEN

Debt Instruments

READING ASSIGNMENT

Chapter 23 Municipal Bonds and Notes
Chapter 24 U.S. Treasury Bills, Notes, and Bonds

OBJECTIVES

- To list the types of municipal bonds.
- To describe how bonds are traded and priced.
- To identify the three forms of securities the Fed issues.

READING ORIENTATION

Municipal bonds, or munis, are debt instruments issued by state and local governments to raise capital to finance their projects and other needs. Details regarding this type of instrument are covered in Chapter 23.

The U.S. government is a *primary participant* in the securities marketplace. The methods by which the government carries out its monetary policy are briefly discussed in Chapter 24.

KEY TERMS

BAN, 202
Book-entry system, 206
Dealer's broker, 201
Discount, 204
Discounted instrument, 202
General obligation, 201
Limited tax, 201
Municipal bonds, 190–191
Primary dealer, 204
RAN, 202
Revenue bonds, 201
Secondary market, 198
Serial bond, 202
TAN, 202
Thin trading, 198
Tight, 206
U.S. Treasury bill, 203, 204–205
U.S. Treasury bond, 203, 205
U.S. Treasury note, 203, 205

Challenge

MATCHING QUIZ

Match each term at the left with a definition at the right, by placing the number of the definition in the fill-in space next to the term. There are more definitions than terms. (Each question is worth 3 points.)

_____ **primary dealers**

_____ **discounted instrument**

_____ **limited tax bond**

_____ **municipal bond**

_____ **Treasury note**

_____ **tight**

_____ **serial bonds**

_____ **revenue bond**

_____ **secondary market**

_____ **book-entry system**

1. Debt instrument issued by state and local governments to raise capital.

2. The spread between a bid and offer is small.

3. Privately-owned firms registered as dealers.

4. Secured by the revenue from the project built by capital raised in the bond issue.

5. The rate of interest is built into the discount.

6. An intermediate-debt instrument of the federal government, issued in coupon or interest rate form.

7. Delivery of a transaction is made through computer entry.

8. TANs, RANs, and BANs.

9. OTC.

10. Backed by a state sales tax.

11. Several bonds maturing at different times.

12. The lower the price, the higher the yield.

MULTIPLE CHOICE

Select the letter that best answers the numbered question. (Each question is worth 4 points.)

1. Municipal bonds are issued by:

I. the federal government
II. the state government
III. the city government
IV. the town government
V. a foreign government

a) I only
b) II only
c) II and III
d) II, III and IV
e) V only

2. A key feature of many municipal bonds is that:

a) they are backed by the federal government
b) interest paid is free from federal income tax
c) any earnings are free from federal taxes
d) the individual issues have adjustable interest rates
e) they are short-term instruments

3. Which of the following are discount instruments?

a) U.S. Treasury bills
b) U.S. Treasury bonds
c) municipal bonds
d) corporate bonds
e) Treasury stock

4. A bond secured by the full taxing-power of the issuing state or local government is called a:

a) revenue bond
b) limited tax bond
c) general obligation bond
d) treasury bond
e) amortized bond

5. Generally speaking, it is difficult to acquire a specific municipal bond issue in the:

a) auction market
b) secondary market
c) brokerage firm
d) branch office
e) AMEX

6. Bids submitted by dealers for an issue must be:

a) in line with current market conditions
b) short term
c) premium
d) discounted
e) long term

7. Bonds are issued with maturities ranging from:

a) 1–10 years
b) 10–20 years
c) 20–30 years
d) 10–30 years
e) 20–40 years

8. When state and local authorities issue short-term instruments in anticipation of taxes received, these are called:

- **a)** TANs
- **b)** BANs
- **c)** RANs
- **d)** notes
- **e)** discounted instruments

9. Purchasers usually buy municipal bonds for:

- **a)** dividends
- **b)** investment purposes
- **c)** frequent trading
- **d)** ongoing trading
- **e)** taxable interest payments

10. Long-term financing can be found in the form of:

- **a)** T-bills
- **b)** munis
- **c)** T-notes
- **d)** RANs
- **e)** T-bonds

TRUE/FALSE

Questions 11–22 are either true or false. Mark T for true, F for false. (Each question is worth 2½ points.)

11. Another term for basis price, as used in municipal securities and other debt instruments, is yield to maturity. ______

12. A municipal bond backed by the ability of the issue to collect income is known as a revenue bond. ______

13. Discounted instruments can best be represented by U.S. Treasury bonds. ______

14. A discount price gives the buyer an increased-dollar yield to maturity. ______

15. Dealer earn their income from the number of trades in one day. ______

16. The public purchases U.S. Treasuries directly from the auction market. ______

17. U.S. Treasury bills are long-term instruments with the longest maturity of 10 years. ______

18. A dealer's broker acts as an intermediary between prospective buying and selling firms. ______

19. Municipalities' debt instruments compete for public funds with other fixed-income securities. ______

20. When municipals are offered, brokerage firms buy the issue from managers. ______

21. The rule in basis pricing is the lower the price, the higher the yield. ______

22. Interest for treasury bonds and notes is computed on a 365-day basis. ______

Answer Sheet

Matching Quiz

3 primary dealers
5 discounted instrument
10 limited tax bond
1 municipal bond
6 Treasury note
2 tight
11 serial bonds
4 revenue bond
9 secondary market
7 book-entry system

Multiple Choice

1. d
2. b
3. a
4. c
5. b
6. a
7. d
8. a
9. b
10. e

True/False

11. T
12. T
13. F
14. T
15, F
16. F
17. F
18. T
19. T
20. F
21. T
22. T

LESSON ELEVEN

Mortgage-Backed Securities, Commercial Paper, Banker's Acceptances, and Certificates of Deposit

READING ASSIGNMENT

Chapter 25	Mortgage-backed Securities
Chapter 26	Commercial Paper
Chapter 27	Banker's Acceptance (BA)
Chapter 28	Certificates of Deposit (CDs)

OBJECTIVES

- To understand the differences between GNMAs, commercial paper, BAs, and CDs.
- To list hedging vehicles used in mortgage-backed securities.
- To know how certificates are handled.
- To identify the types of CDs.

READING ORIENTATION

This lesson deals with other types of securities available to the investor of which the securities-industry employee should become aware. *Mortgage-backed securities,* known as GNMAs, are debt instruments that represent pooled mortgages. They are discussed in Chapter 25.

Commercial paper, covered in Chapter 26, is a short-term debt instrument that is offered by corporations. Its rate of interest is set at issuance and can be realized only if held to maturity.

Banker's acceptances, discussed in Chapter 27, are bills of exchange that are issued and guaranteed by a bank for payment within one to six months. They are used to expedite payment of goods in transit between exporting and importing countries.

Certificates of deposit are negotiable securities issued by commercial banks against money deposited over a period of time. Four types of CDs are briefly discussed in Chapter 28.

KEY TERMS

Banker's acceptance, 217
Call, 211
Certificate of deposit, 219
Collateralized loan, 215
Commercial paper, 213
Dealer-sold paper, 214
Direct placement, 214
Discounted instrument, 213
Domestic CD, 219
Eurodollar CD, 220
Factor table, 211
Fed wire, 214
Fixed payment mortgage, 212
Futures contract, 211
Ginnie Maes, 207
Graduated payment mortgage, 212
Money-market instrument, 218
Mortgage banker, 209
Participating certificate, 210
Pass-through certificates, 207
Plus interest instrument, 213
Pool number, 210
Repo, 215
Reserve requirement, 218
Standby, 211
TBA, 210
TBA GNMA contract, 209
Yankee CD, 220

Challenge

MATCHING QUIZ

Match each term at the left with a definition at the right, by placing the number of the definition in the fill-in space next to the term. There are more definitions than terms. (Each question is worth 2½ points.)

_____ **standby**

_____ **yankee CD**

_____ **money-market instrument**

_____ **direct placement**

_____ **Fed wire**

_____ **commercial paper**

_____ **participating certificate**

_____ **certificate of deposit**

_____ **banker's acceptance**

_____ **plus interest payment**

_____ **pool number**

_____ **factor table**

1. Takes place between a bank and its customers.

2. Based on a bank's pooled-mortgages.

3. Number assigned by GNMA to a specific group of mortgages once all the mortgages are enforced.

4. Permits a holder to sell a specified amount of certificates at a set price for a given period.

5. Debt instrument that is sometimes offered as a discount instrument.

6. Corporate short-term loans.

7. Bills of exchange issued and guaranteed by a bank for payment within one to six months.

8. Issued to investors by U.S. branches of foreign banks.

9. A communications network.

10. The client pays the full face value to buy the paper and receives the face value plus the interest accrued at maturity.

11. Short-term debt of banks.

12. Includes U.S. T-bills, commercial paper, and banker's acceptances.

13. Used in adjustment of mortgage balances.

14. Permits a holder to buy a specified amount of certificates at a set price for a given period.

MULTIPLE CHOICE

Select the letter that best answers the numbered question. (Each question is worth 4 points.)

1. The shortest-term corporate debt issued is:

a) stock
b) rights
c) bonds
d) notes
e) commercial paper

2. An instrument that typically pays principal and interest to its owners on a monthly basis is known as:

- **a)** T-bills
- **b)** Commercial paper
- **c)** GNMAs
- **d)** Options
- **e)** T-bonds

3. A short-term debt issued by banks and used in international trade is:

- **a)** stock
- **b)** bond
- **c)** banker's acceptance
- **d)** commercial paper
- **e)** mortgage-backed security

4. CDs are primarily resold in what market?

- **a)** auction
- **b)** OTC
- **c)** foreign
- **d)** commodities
- **e)** option

5. In mortgage-backed securities, a standby, call, and futures contract are considered what kind of vehicles?

- **a)** trading
- **b)** selling
- **c)** buying
- **d)** hedging
- **e)** figuring

6. In the case of a discounted instrument,

- **a)** dividends are paid
- **b)** interest payments are made
- **c)** no interest payments are made
- **d)** interest is accrued
- **e)** face value is increased

7. Transactions in commercial paper settle:

a) next day
b) same day
c) T + 2
d) T + 3
e) T + 4

8. In which marketplace are pass-through securities traded?

a) brokerage firms
b) banks
c) NYSE
d) AMEX
e) OTC

9. In which instrument does the following apply?

The interest earned is the difference between what investors pay (for the instrument) and the face value they are paid at maturity.

a) CD
b) GNMA
c) GPM
d) BA
e) PC

10. A GNMA dealer has an inventory of $10,000,000 in a particular security. Presently, it is trading at 80, but the dealer fears a drop in price. To protect the value of the inventory, what should the dealer do?

a) pay a premium for a standby
b) pay a discount for a standby
c) pay interest
d) sell early
e) renegotiate the trade

TRUE/FALSE

Questions 11–22 are either true or false. Mark T for true, F for false. (Each question is worth 2½ points.)

11. GNMAs are brought to market through negotiated underwriting. ______

12. The current outstanding principal of a mortgage backed pass-through can be obtained through the use of the factor table. ______

13. Short-term debt instruments of corporations are known as notes. ______

14. Banks involved with international commerce may issue banker's acceptances for financing purposes. ______

15. Short-term debt instruments issued by banks are certificates of deposit. ______

16. Interest is paid through the life of the mortgage on a fixed payment mortgage. ______

17. If a dealer buys and resells paper on the trade date, the paper has to be financed. ______

18. The interest on CDs is computed on a 365-day basis. ______

19. Commercial paper trading lots are $1,000,000. ______

20. Domestic CDs are issued by American banks to investors in foreign countries. ______

21. Mortgage bankers arrange financing for buyers of homes and project housing in money-sparce areas. ______

22. The monthly payments received from the mortgagees are all interest. ______

Answer Sheet

Matching Quiz

4 standby
8 yankee CD
12 money-market instrument
1 direct placement
9 Fed wire
6 commercial paper
2 participating certificate
11 certificate of deposit
7 banker's acceptance
10 plus interest payment
3 pool number
13 factor table

Multiple Choice

1. e
2. c
3. c
4. b
5. d
6. c
7. b
8. e
9. d
10. a

True/False

11. F
12. T
13. F
14. T
15. T
16. T
17. F
18. F
19. T
20. F
21. T
22. F

LESSON TWELVE

Mutual Funds, Options, and Futures

READING ASSIGNMENT

Chapter 29 Mutual Funds
Chapter 30 Options
Chapter 31 Futures

OBJECTIVES

- To identify the types of mutual funds.
- To understand how options operate.
- To describe the concept of futures contracts.

READING ORIENTATION

Mutual funds can be many types of funds including growth, income, bond, common stock, and so on. Each type of fund attempts to acquire securities that best fill its goals, thereby benefiting its shareowners. This is discussed in Chapter 29.

Options are contracts that entitle the owner to buy or sell a security at a certain price before a certain date. There are basically two types of options, a *call* and *put*. These and other types of options are discussed in Chapter 30.

Futures are long-term contracts on underlying instruments such as grain or precious metal, by which the buyer and seller lock in a price for a later delivery.

KEY TERMS

As-of, 233
Assign, 226
Breakpoint, 223
Broker, 233
Call, 226
Closed-end fund, 222
Contractual plan, 222
Daily-trading limits, 235
Debits, 234
Delivery notices, 234
Excess, 234
Exercise, 226
Expiration date, 226
Futures, 232–233
Holder, 226
Index option, 229
Letter of intent, 222
Listed option, 227
Load fund, 223
Long position, 233
Market-weighted, 229
Money market, 225
Mutual fund, 221
Net asset value, 222
No-load fund, 224
OCC, 230
Open-end fund, 221
Option, 226
Outright purchase, 221
Owner, 226
Put, 226
Quote, 224
Rejected trade notice, 233
Rights of accumulation, 222
ROTN, 230
Share-weighted, 229
Short position, 233
Standard margin, 234
Strike price, 226
Underlying security, 226
Units, 224
Variation margin, 234
Voluntary plan, 222
Writer, 226

Challenge

MATCHING QUIZ

Match each term at the left with a definition at the right, by placing the number of the definition in the fill-in space next to the term. There are more definitions than terms. (Each question is worth 2 points.)

_____ **money-market fund**

_____ **long position**

_____ **growth fund**

_____ **standard margin**

_____ **load**

_____ **tax-free fund**

_____ **breakpoint**

_____ **short position**

_____ **open end**

_____ **market-weighted**

_____ **rights of accumulation**

_____ **call option**

_____ **OCC**

1. Invests in young or emerging companies.

2. Fund makes a continuous offering of its shares to the public.

3. Amount of sales charge.

4. Gives the owner the privilege of buying an option.

5. Invests in different foreign currencies.

6. Selling a futures contract.

7. Invests in municipal securities.

8. Where member firms must settle the net cash differences from their daily activity and deposit the required position margin.

9. Buying a futures contract.

10. The number of shares outstanding or listed on an exchange is multiplied by the current market price.

11. Amount required per contract position on futures transactions.

12. Common stock fund.

13. Point at which the percentage of a fee drops.

14. Sales charge percent decreases as amount invested grows.

15. Invests in short-term instruments.

MULTIPLE CHOICE

Select the letter that best answers the numbered question. (Each question is worth 5 points.)

1. An instrument that gives its owner the privilege of buying an underlying security any time during the instrument's life is a:

a) stock
b) bond
c) call option
d) put option
e) future

2. The instrument that sets the price at which a delivery will take place at a much later date is a:

- **a)** put option
- **b)** call option
- **c)** future
- **d)** corporate bond
- **e)** commercial paper

3. In a contractual plan, the sales charge is based on:

- **a)** the prime rate
- **b)** the total amount contracted for
- **c)** half the amount contracted for
- **d)** a letter of intent
- **e)** the interest rate

4. In listed options, equity options are usually issued in the following intervals:

- **a)** one-, two-, and three-month
- **b)** two-, four-, and six-month
- **c)** three-, six-, and nine-month
- **d)** three-, six-, and nine-week
- **e)** one-, three-, and six-week

5. Standard and variation margins are charged on what types of transactions?

- **a)** futures
- **b)** options
- **c)** stock
- **d)** OTC
- **e)** mutual funds

6. What has to be reached in order to reduce the sales charge under rights of accumulation?

- **a)** agreement
- **b)** a negotiable contract
- **c)** the net asset value
- **d)** the breakpoint
- **e)** the deadline

7. In listed options, the exchanges use a formula to establish strike prices. Generally, equity options with strike prices from $25 to $200 are issued in:

a) $5 variations
b) $10 variations
c) $20 variations
d) 2½ point multiples
e) 1 point multiple

8. During the last month of their contract life, futures become known as:

a) stocks
b) bonds
c) options
d) units
e) spot month

9. When an index is share-weighted, all common stocks are usually based on:

a) 10-share units
b) index value
c) net asset value
d) 100-share units
e) current market price

10. What does the following statement describe?

The bid represents the net asset value, the offer is the net asset value plus the maximum sales charge.

a) index option
b) futures
c) load fund
d) closed-end fund
e) call option

TRUE/FALSE

Questions 11–22 are either true or false. Mark T for true, F for false. (Each question is worth 2 points.)

11. The pooling of money in a managed company to achieve certain objectives is the purpose of a mutual fund. ______

12. Net asset value is the "bid" side of an open-end mutual funds quote. ______

13. Closed-end mutual funds carry load charges. ______

14. The price at which an option can be exercised is known as its call price. ______

15. In listed options, strike prices are set by the brokerage firm. ______

16. The margin required by clearing corporations is constant. ______

17. For load funds, the offer is higher than the bid. ______

18. Options may be used by hedgers to protect against a loss in stock that they own. ______

19. An index option is an option on a bond index. ______

20. Option positions that are not traded out or exercised, eventually are renewed. ______

21. In futures, trades not compared on the night of trade date are known as rejected trade notices or out trades. ______

22. In an outright purchase, the client invests a fixed sum of money. ______

Answer Sheet

Matching Quiz

15 money-market fund
9 long position
1 growth fund
11 standard margin
3 load
7 tax-free fund
13 breakpoint
6 short position
2 open-end
10 market-weighted
14 rights of accumulation
4 call option
8 OCC

Multiple Choice

1. c
2. c
3. b
4. c
5. a
6. d
7. a
8. e
9. d
10. c

True/False

11. T
12. T
13. F
14. F
15. F
16. F
17. T
18. T
19. F
20. F
21. T
22. T

Midterm

MATCHING QUIZ

Match each term at the left with a definition at the right, by placing the number of the definition in the fill-in space next to the term. There are more definitions than terms. (Each question is worth 1 point.)

_____ **service bureau**

_____ **proprietorship**

_____ **stock split**

_____ **fed fund**

_____ **cash dividend**

_____ **stock dividend**

_____ **corporation**

_____ **subject quote**

_____ **rights**

_____ **asset**

_____ **figuration**

_____ **auction market**

_____ **contract sheet**

_____ **buying power**

_____ **daily cash report**

_____ **municipal bond**

_____ **market order**

_____ **proxy**

_____ **lending agreement**

_____ **theoretical value**

_____ **secondary market**

_____ **underwriting**

_____ **specialist**

_____ **money market instruments**

_____ **regulation T**

1. Simplest form of business.

2. Enables the shareholder to vote for members of management and other key issues affecting the corporation.

3. Listing of trade information from both buyer and seller firms.

4. Sets highest price to pay or lowest price to receive.

5. Price at which the trader believes the trade can be consummated.

6. Holders receive one or more shares of additional issue for each share held.

7. Paid as a percentage of shares owned.

8. Process by which securities are first brought to the market.

9. The difference between the subscription price and the market price divided by the number of rights required to purchase one new share.

10. Customer monies computation.

11. Money movements that occurred in the firm on the previous day.

12. Maintains fair and orderly markets in stocks assigned to them.

13. The dollar amount worth of securities that can be purchased without depositing additional funds.

14. When only one side of an entry is recorded.

15. Backbone of all margin rules.

16. Permission for a firm to lend margined securities to other firms or against other customers' short sales.

17. Same-day money.

18. A security that gives stockholders the opportunity to purchase additional shares in proportion to their present holdings.

19. Debt instrument issued by state and local governments to raise capital.

20. A company that specializes in computer processing.

21. Highest bid and lowest offer have priority.

22. Includes U.S. T-bills, commercial paper, and banker's acceptances.

23. Life of the business is separate from that of the owners.

24. Accepts current price.

25. Inventory.

26. Paid on a per-share basis.

27. OTC.

MULTIPLE CHOICE

Select the letter that best answers the numbered question. (Each question is worth 2 points.)

1. The ability of a single proprietor to raise funds is based on the worth of the:

a) individual
b) business
c) shareholders
d) limited partners
e) all of the above

2. The formal document used to attract other firms into the underwriting is known as the:

a) final prospectus
b) book of forms
c) preliminary prospectus
d) offering circular
e) book offering

3. Which of the following securities trade over-the-counter?

a) common stock
b) preferred stock
c) corporate bond
d) municipal bond
e) all of the above

4. Compute the current yield on the following bond:

$1,000 RAM 10% – FA – 2006 = 90 ($900)

The current yield is:

a) 10 percent
b) 9 percent
c) 9.26 percent
d) 11.11 percent
e) 12.25 percent

5. Which of the following must be on a customer's confirmation?

I. bought or sold

II. quantity and price

III. security description

IV. trade date and settlement date

V. place of execution

a) I, II, IV

b) I, II, III

c) III, IV, V

d) I, III, V

e) I, II, III, IV, V

6. The responsibility for maintaining customer accounts in accordance with the various rules and regulations belongs to the:

a) P&S department

b) transfer department

c) margin department

d) dividend department

e) stock record department

7. Recording and balancing of all security movements within the firm is the responsibility of the:

a) P&S department

b) margin department

c) cashiers department

d) stock record department

e) dividend department

8. Customers whose stock is registered in the firm's name,

a) lose their right to vote

b) will be notified how the firm voted the stock

c) will vote by proxies sent to them by the firm

d) may receive a pass from the firm to attend corporate meetings

e) may vote only if the stock pays a dividend

9. Margin accounts require which of the following sets of papers?

I. new accounts form
II. margin agreement
III. trust agreement
IV. loan agreement
V. custody agreement

a) I and IV
b) I, II and IV
c) II, III and IV
d) I, IV and V
e) II, IV and V

10. WIP common stock is trading at $30 per share; the corporate bond $1,000 WIP 8% FA—2006 is convertible into 25 shares of common stock. What would the bond be selling at if it were at parity?

a) $1,000
b) $800
c) $750
d) $500
e) $1,200

11. A key feature of most municipal bonds is that:

a) they are backed by the federal government
b) interest paid is free from federal income tax
c) any earnings are free from federal taxes
d) the individual issues have adjustable interest rates
e) they are short-term instruments

12. The shortest-term corporate debt issued is:

a) stock
b) rights
c) bonds
d) notes
e) commercial paper

13. An instrument that gives its owner the privilege of buying an underlying security any time during the instrument's life is a:

- **a)** stock
- **b)** bond
- **c)** call option
- **d)** put option
- **e)** future

14. The order room function includes the matching of a report with the original order and then advising the account executive. What is this report called?

- **a)** pending
- **b)** execution
- **c)** marketing
- **d)** functional
- **e)** bid

15. What is one of the main functions of the cashiering department?

- **a)** borrowing and lending money
- **b)** vaulting
- **c)** receiving
- **d)** delivering
- **e)** all of the above

16. The balance sheet is set up so that the total of assets equals:

- **a)** the difference between the liabilities and net worth
- **b)** the sum of total liabilities and net worth
- **c)** the sum of the income and expenses
- **d)** all the expenses
- **e)** none of the above

17. Settled positions include which of the following?

a) securities bought and paid for, but not in good deliverable form or not sold

b) physical inventory owned

c) securities sold but not delivered

d) all of the above

e) none of the above

18. On commercial loans, banks charge a rate of interest based on:

a) the minimum margin requirement

b) the prime lending rate

c) the Reg-T requirement

d) the dividend value

e) the cash value of the security

19. If a common stock is registered in the name of the firm or a bank (in behalf of the owner), then it is registered in:

a) the beneficial owner's behalf

b) the OTC market

c) the customer's name

d) street name

e) round lots

20. Bonds are issued with maturities ranging from:

a) 1–10 years

b) 10–20 years

c) 20–30 years

d) 10–30 years

e) 20–40 years

21. What entitles a holder to convert a security into common stock at a set price during a specified period of time?

- **a)** a unit
- **b)** a right
- **c)** a warrant
- **d)** a bond
- **e)** a convertible preferred

22. What has the most influence on income-bearing, or fixed-dividend securities?

- **a)** bond prices
- **b)** interest rate fluctuations
- **c)** dividends
- **d)** coupon rate
- **e)** length of ownership

23. A GNMA dealer has an inventory of $10,000,000 in a particular security. Presently, it is trading at 80, but the dealer fears a drop in price. To protect the value of the inventory, what must the dealer do?

- **a)** pay a premium for a standby
- **b)** pay a discount for a standby
- **c)** pay interest
- **d)** sell early
- **e)** renegotiate the trade

24. In listed options, equity options are usually issued in the following intervals:

- **a)** one-, two-, and three-month
- **b)** two-, four-, and six-month
- **c)** three-, six-, and nine-month
- **d)** three-, six-, and nine-week
- **e)** one-, three-, and six-week

25. If a corporation and its investment banker believe that the price of the company's common stock is likely to rise over time, what may they offer?

a) a callable issue

b) a convertible preferred

c) a cumulative preferred

d) a cash dividend

e) a participating preferred

TRUE/FALSE

The following questions are either true or false. Mark T for true, F for false. (Each question is worth 1 point.)

1. Most corporate issues are brought to market through a form of underwriting known as negotiated underwriting. ______

2. The clause in a corporate charter that gives present share-owners the ability to purchase additional shares before nonshare-holders can acquire them is known as preemptive rights. ______

3. Another name for basis price is current yield. ______

4. On a sell trade, commission is added to the trade monies to arrive at the net the client is to receive. ______

5. Securities that a brokerage firm pledges at a bank to secure funds for margin accounts are known as hypothecated securities. ______

6. In establishing a customer account, a limited power of attorney permits the holder of such a power to withdraw and deposit funds and securities. ______

7. Par value of a stock is the same as the market value. ______

8. The process by which bonds are retired through the issuance of new debt instruments is known as refunding. ______

9. A municipal bond backed by the ability of the issue to collect income is known as a revenue bond. ______

10. Banks involved with international commerce may issue banker's acceptances for financing purposes. ______

11. Closed-end mutual funds carry load charges. ______

12. The procedure on the AMEX for awarding trades is known as priority pro rata. ______

13. Part of the booking procedure is the recording of fees and commissions due to the firm. ______

14. Equity = Current Market Value − Debit balance. ______

15. To properly record the movement of securities, the stock record must balance debits versus assets. ______

16. Balance sheets contain all the debits and credits in the adjusted trial balance. ______

17. The compliance department employees make certain that brokers are correctly registered for the type of business they are conducting. ______

18. Firms that deal in government securities turn to other firms for their cashiering function. ______

19. Securities in customers' long and short positions are in a settled position. ______

20. The market price of preferred stock is based on current yield rates for fixed income investments. ______

21. Holders of warrants are initially entitled to a purchase price that is higher than the stock's current market price. ______

22. U.S. Treasury bills are long-term instruments with the longest maturity of 10 years. ______

23. Commercial paper trading lots are $1,000,000. ______

24. Options may be used by hedgers to protect against a loss in stock that they own. ______

25. Warrants are shorter-term issues than rights. ______

Answer Sheet

Matching Quiz

20 service bureau
1 proprietorship
6 stock split
17 fed fund
26 cash dividend
7 stock dividend
23 corporation
5 subject quote
18 rights
25 asset
10 figuration
21 auction market
3 contract sheet
13 buying power
11 daily cash report
19 municipal bond
24 market order
2 proxy
16 lending agreement
9 theoretical value
27 secondary market
8 underwriting
12 specialist
22 certificate of deposit
15 regulation T

Multiple Choice

1. a
2. c
3. e
4. d
5. e
6. c
7. d
8. c
9. b
10. c
11. b
12. e
13. c

14. b
15. e
16. b
17. d
18. b
19. d
20. d
21. e
22. b
23. a
24. c
25. b

True/False

1. T
2. T
3. F
4. F
5. T
6. F
7. F
8. T
9. T
10. T
11. F
12. T
13. T
14. T
15. F
16. F
17. T
18. F
19. F
20. T
21. T
22. F
23. T
24. T
25. F

LESSON THIRTEEN

The Order Room

READING ASSIGNMENT

Chapter 32 Order Room
(review Chapter 6)

OBJECTIVES

- To understand the flow of execution of an order.
- To be able to identify and fill out simple order forms.

READING ORIENTATION

The material covered in this lesson deals entirely with *the order room,* which accepts orders and routes them for execution to either the appropriate exchange or the market maker. Types of orders and the forms needed to carry out these orders are discussed and illustrated. Details regarding problem trades, new trades, and adjusted trades are also discussed.

Some of the information may be familiar to you because it was covered in Lesson 3.

KEY TERMS

Adds and outs, 252
All-or-none, 248
As-of date, 249
Buy at the market, 242
Day order, 244
Do not increase, 251
Do not reduce, 251
Fill-or-kill, 248
GTC order, 244–245
Immediate-or-cancel, 248
Limit order, 243
Market order, 242
Not-held, 248
Nothing done, 251–252
Odd lot, 252–253
Open order, 244
Order room, 241
Round lot, 252–253
Sell at the market, 242
Short sale, 245
Specialist firm, 253
Stop limit order, 247–248
Stop order, 246–247
Volatile issue, 247–248

Challenge

MATCHING QUIZ

Match each term at the left with a definition at the right, by placing the number of the definition in the fill-in space next to the term. There are more definitions than terms. (Each question is worth 3 points.)

_____ **market order**

_____ **AON order**

_____ **add buy**

_____ **stop order**

_____ **buy at the market**

_____ **specialist firm**

_____ **short sale**

_____ **volatile issue**

_____ **as-of date**

_____ **nothing done**

1. Price fluctuates considerably.

2. A memorandum order.

3. Accepts best price at time of entry.

4. Response to orders not entitled to a report

5. Sell a security that is borrowed.

6. Refers to the exchange market.

7. Buys or sells round lots in the open market to offset inventory imbalances.

8. Notification of a pending GTC buy order.

9. Informs all parties of the day that the trade should have taken place.

10. Must complete order execution or client may reject portion completed.

11. Standard unit of trading.

12. Willing to accept the lowest offer.

MULTIPLE CHOICE

Select the letter that best answers the numbered question. (Each question is worth 4 points.)

1. Upon arriving at work in the order room in the morning, Phil O'Dendrin, an employee of SF&R, discovers a trade from the day before has not been processed. Phil should:

a) throw out the trade

b) cancel the trade

c) process the trade "as-of"

d) process the trade as if it were executed today

e) wait for the market to open to see if a "better" price can be obtained

2. The employee, Phil, then receives a report request from one of SF&R's branches. A limit order had been entered yesterday at 2:32 P.M. (EST) to buy 100 POP at 32. He checks "time & sales" and discovers the following information:

	TIME	*TRADE*	*QUOTE (new)*
	10:26	300 at 31½	31½–32
	12:30	100 at 32	31⅞–32⅛
	1:05	400 at 32⅛	32 –32¼
	1:45	200 at 32¼	32¼–32½
	2:03	100 at 32½	32⅝–32⅞
	2:41	200 at 32⅞	32¾–33
	3:00	100 at 33	32¾–33
(last sale)	3:29	400 at 33	32⅞–33⅛

What price should the customer receive?

a) nothing can be done
b) 32
c) 31½
d) 32⅞
e) 33

3. Regarding question 2, if the order has been a market order instead of a limit order, what price would the customer be entitled to?

a) 32½
b) 32⅝
c) 32⅞
d) 33
e) the "high" price for the day

4. A customer's instructions to buy or sell a security are written out on:

a) a blotter
b) a report
c) an order form
d) a contract
e) a memorandum

5. Which type of transaction permits you to make a profit from falling stock prices?

a) market order
b) limit order
c) GTC order
d) as-of sale
e) short sale

Questions 6–10 require the completion of SF&R's order forms which have been provided starting on page 120. Each correct form is worth four points. To fill out the forms, the following information is provided:

A/C #ZA218924 - Mr. Wynn Doe - Cash account = Type 1
A/C #ZA220345 - Ms. Della Kettesin - Margin account = Type 2
A/C #ZA240491 - Mr. John Hill - Margin account = Type 2
A/C #ZA240492 - Mr. John Hill & Jill Hill - JTROS cash account = Type 1

The security is the Ripemhoff Surgical Supply Company, symbol RIP, traded on the NYSE. The current quote is 34-¼, last sale 34⅛, preceding sale 34¼. RIP is traded on the NYSE. (Pertains to questions 6–8 only.)

Your are the stockbroker. Your ID is ZA041. Based on the following customer's instructions, complete the order forms.

6. Customer Wynn Doe, after discussing RIP, says "Buy me 200 shares at the offer."

7. Customer Della Kettesin, after discussing RIP, says "I have $7,000 in my margin account. Buy me whatever round lots you can."

8. Customer John Hill, after discussing RIP, says "Buy 200 at 34 in my joint account and 300 at the market in my personal account. Make the 200-share order an open order."

9. Later in the day, you are speaking with Della, and she wants to sell 25,000 shares Loster Motor Corp. (symbol LMC), which is presently trading on the NYSE at $27 per share. As the large block may upset the market, she instructs you to tell your floor broker to take his/her time and release the stock gradually.

10. In a subsequent conversation with John Hill, you discover that he is nervous about some news on the Randis Corp. trading on the Pacific Stock Exchange at $32. He currently owns 400 shares in his personal account and does not want to sell the security. If it should ever fall in value to $30, however, he wants the stock sold. The symbol for Randis is RAN. Prepare the order that accomplishes this goal.

6

	STOCK EXCHANGES						BONDS			BLOCK DEPT	FINAN. SERV DEPT.	SYNDI-CATE	MUTUAL FUNDS	SPECIAL HANDLING	OTHER	ORDER NUMBER	OFFICE	EXECUTED PRICE
	NYSE & ASE	NASDAQ	OVER THE CNTR	CHI'GO MID-WEST	PACIFIC COAST	BOSTON P-B-W	CORP-ORATE	MUNI-CIPAL	CONV-ERTIBLE									
0	☐ NAX	☐ OTC	☐ OTN	☐ CMW	☐ PCX	☐ HEND	☐ BND	☐ BMUN	☐ CONV	☐ ID	☐ FND	☐ STIC	☐ CGE	☐ SHD				

B U Y

1 ☐ POSS DUPE ☐ BUY ATTN:

2 QUANTITY | SYMBOL OR DESCRIPTION | SUFFIX* | PRICE OR MARKET | STOP ☐ STP | STOP LIMIT PRICE ______LMT | TYPE OF ORDER OTHER THAN LIMITED OR MARKET ☐ BAS ☐ OB ☐ WITH DISCRETION ☐ WOW ☐ CLO

3 ☐ AON ☐ NH ☐ DAY ☐ GTC ☐ OPG ☐ FOK ☐ OC ☐ DNR ☐ CASH ☐ ND | PRINCIPAL TRANSACTION

4 ☐ POSS DUPE ☐ OR ☐ SW ☐ CXL ☐ BUY | ☐ INFORM CUSTOMER WE MAKE MARKET

5 QUANTITY | SYMBOL OR DESCRIPTION | SUFFIX* | PRICE OR MARKET | STOP ☐ STP | STOP LIMIT PRICE ______LMT | ☐ BAS ☐ OB ☐ WITH DISCRETION ☐ WOW ☐ CLO

6 LVS ☐ AON ☐ NH ☐ DAY ☐ GTC ☐ OPG ☐ FOK ☐ OC ☐ DNR ☐ CASH ☐ ND ☐ CHECK IF NEW ACCOUNT

7 OFFICE | ACCOUNT NUMBER | TYPE | TYPE OF ACCOUNT | SPLIT SHARES | DISCRETIONARY NYSE RULE 408 | EMPLOYEE | A.E. NO. | MGR'S. APPROVAL

TYPE OF ACCOUNT:
0 - COD
1 - CASH
2 - MARGIN
3 - SHORT
4 - SPEC. SUBSCRIPTION
5 - CONV. BOND
6 - SPEC. BOND

8 CXL'S ONLY | REF | ORIG STATION | MESSAGE NO. | CUSTOMER NAME

9 COM ☐ A.E. OVERRIDE [R/___] ☐ NEG. ¢ PER SH [M/90 ___] ☐ NEG. DISC. [CD__%] ☐ ST INS OVERRIDE [I/_]

10 COM ☐ SPECIAL DESCRIPTIVE INST. [D/______________________________] ☐ D/UNSOL

11 COM

12 COM

13 CONFIRM LINE CFN LINE 2 & 5

ORDER COPY

SUFFIX CODES

CALLED CL
CERTIFICATE . CT
CLASS OF ... AB
SECURITY . ETC.
CONVERTIBLE CV
FOREIGN . ... F
PREFERRED ... PR
RIGHTS ... RT
SPECIAL ... SP
STAMPED .. SD
WHEN DISTRIBUTED . WD
WHEN ISSUED ... WI
WITH WARRANTS .. WW
WITHOUT WARRANTS . XW
WARRANTS . WS

7

B U Y

SUFFIX CODES

CALLED CL
CERTIFICATE . CT
CLASS OF ... AB
SECURITY . ETC.
CONVERTIBLE CV
FOREIGN ..... F
PREFERRED PR
RIGHTS RT
SPECIAL SP
STAMPED .. SD
WHEN DISTRIBUTED . WD
WHEN ISSUED ... WI
WITH WARRANTS .. WW
WITHOUT WARRANTS . XW
WARRANTS . WS

0 STOCK EXCHANGES: NYSE & ASE ☐ NAX | NASDAQ ☐ OTC | OVER THE CNTR ☐ OTN | CHI'GO MID-WEST ☐ CMW | PACIFIC COAST ☐ PCX | BOSTON P-B-W ☐ HEND
BONDS: CORP-ORATE ☐ BND | MUNI-CIPAL ☐ BMUN | CONV-ERTIBLE ☐ CONV
BLOCK DEPT ☐ ID | FINAN. SERV DEPT. ☐ FND | SYNDI-CATE ☐ STIC | MUTUAL FUNDS ☐ CGE | SPECIAL HAND'NG ☐ SHD | OTHER | ORDER NUMBER | OFFICE | EXECUTED PRICE

1 ☐ POSS DUPE | ☐ BUY | ATTN:

2 QUANTITY | SYMBOL OR DESCRIPTION | SUFFIX* | PRICE OR MARKET | STOP ☐ STP | STOP LIMIT PRICE ____LMT | TYPE OF ORDER OTHER THAN LIMITED OR MARKET ☐ BAS ☐ OB ☐ WITH DISCRETION ☐ WOW ☐ CLO

3 ☐ AON ☐ N H | ☐ DAY ☐ GTC ☐ OPG ☐ FOK ☐ OC | ☐ DNR ☐ CASH ☐ ND | PRINCIPAL TRANSACTION

4 ☐ POSS DUPE | ☐ OR ☐ SW ☐ CXL ☐ BUY | ☐ INFORM CUSTOMER WE MAKE MARKET

5 QUANTITY | SYMBOL OR DESCRIPTION | SUFFIX* | PRICE OR MARKET | STOP ☐ STP | STOP LIMIT PRICE ____LMT | ☐ BAS ☐ OB ☐ WITH DISCRETION ☐ WOW ☐ CLO

6 LVS ☐ AON ☐ NH ☐ DAY ☐ GTC ☐ OPG ☐ FOK ☐ OC ☐ DNR ☐ CASH ☐ ND | ☐ CHECK IF NEW ACCOUNT

7 OFFICE | ACCOUNT NUMBER | TYPE | TYPE OF ACCOUNT | SPLIT SHARES | DISCRETIONARY NYSE RULE 408 | EMPLOYEE | A.E. NO. | MGR'S. APPROVAL

TYPE OF ACCOUNT:
0 - COD
1 - CASH
2 - MARGIN
3 - SHORT
4 - SPEC. SUBSCRIPTION
5 - CONV. BOND
6 - SPEC. BOND

8 CXL'S ONLY | REF | ORIG STATION | MESSAGE NO. | CUSTOMER NAME

9 COM | ☐ A.E. OVERRIDE [R/ _ _ _] | ☐ NEG. ¢ PER SH [M/90 _ _ _] | ☐ NEG. DISC [CD _ _ %] | ☐ ST INS OVERRIDE [I/ _]

10 COM | ☐ SPECIAL DESCRIPTIVE INST. [D/ _] | ☐ D/UNSOL

11 COM

12 COM

13 CONFIRM LINE CFN LINE 2 & 5

ORDER COPY

8

BUY

	STOCK EXCHANGES						BONDS			BLOCK DEPT	FINAN. SERV. DEPT.	SYNDI-CATE	MUTUAL FUNDS	SPECIAL HAND'NG	OTHER	ORDER NUMBER	OFFICE	EXECUTED PRICE
	NYSE & ASE	NASDAQ	OVER THE CNTR	CHI'GO MID-WEST	PACIFIC COAST	BOSTON P-B-W	CORP-ORATE	MUNI-CIPAL	CONV-ERTIBLE									
0	☐ NAX	☐ OTC	☐ OTN	☐ CMW	☐ PCX	☐ HEND	☐ BND	☐ BMUN	☐ CONV	☐ ID	☐ FND	☐ STIC	☐ CGE	☐ SHD				

1 ☐ POSS DUPE ☐ **BUY** ATTN:

2 QUANTITY | SYMBOL OR DESCRIPTION | SUFFIX* | PRICE OR MARKET | STOP ☐ STP | STOP LIMIT PRICE ____ LMT | TYPE OF ORDER OTHER THAN LIMITED OR MARKET ☐ BAS ☐ OB ☐ WITH DISCRETION ☐ WOW ☐ CLO

3 ☐ AON ☐ NH ☐ DAY ☐ GTC ☐ OPG ☐ FOK ☐ OC ☐ DNR ☐ CASH ☐ ND | PRINCIPAL TRANSACTION

4 ☐ POSS DUPE ☐ OR ☐ SW ☐ CXL ☐ BUY | ☐ INFORM CUSTOMER WE MAKE MARKET

5 QUANTITY | SYMBOL OR DESCRIPTION | SUFFIX* | PRICE OR MARKET | STOP ☐ STP | STOP LIMIT PRICE ____ LMT | ☐ BAS ☐ OB ☐ WITH DISCRETION ☐ WOW ☐ CLO

6 LVS ☐ AON ☐ NH ☐ DAY ☐ GTC ☐ OPG ☐ FOK ☐ OC ☐ DNR ☐ CASH ☐ ND ☐ CHECK IF NEW ACCOUNT

7 OFFICE | ACCOUNT NUMBER | TYPE | **TYPE OF ACCOUNT** 0-COD 1-CASH 2-MARGIN 3-SHORT 4-SPEC. SUBSCRIPTION 5-CONV. BOND 6-SPEC. BOND | SPLIT SHARES | DISCRETIONARY NYSE RULE 406 | EMPLOYEE | A.E. NO. | MGR'S APPROVAL

8 CXL'S ONLY | REF | ORIG STATION | MESSAGE NO. | CUSTOMER NAME

9 COM ☐ A.E. OVERRIDE [R/___] ☐ NEG. ¢ PER SH [M/90 ___] ☐ NEG. DISC. [CD__%] ☐ ST INS OVERRIDE [I/_]

10 COM ☐ SPECIAL DESCRIPTIVE INST. [D/______________________________] ☐ D/UNSOL

11 COM

12 COM

13 CONFIRM LINE CFN LINE 2 & 5

SUFFIX CODES

CALLED CL
CERTIFICATE . CT
CLASS OF ..... AB
SECURITY . ETC.
CONVERTIBLE CV
FOREIGN ..... F
PREFERRED ... PR
RIGHTS ..... RT
SPECIAL ..... SP
STAMPED ... SD
WHEN DISTRIBUTED . WD
WHEN ISSUED ... WI
WITH WARRANTS .. WW
WITHOUT WARRANTS . XW
WARRANTS . WS

ORDER COPY

BUY

	STOCK EXCHANGES						BONDS			BLOCK DEPT	FINAN. SERV. DEPT.	SYNDI-CATE	MUTUAL FUNDS	SPECIAL HAND'NG	OTHER	ORDER NUMBER	OFFICE	EXECUTED PRICE
	NYSE & ASE	NASDAQ	OVER THE CNTR	CHI'GO MID-WEST	PACIFIC COAST	BOSTON P-B-W	CORP-ORATE	MUNI-CIPAL	CONV-ERTIBLE									
0	☐ NAX	☐ OTC	☐ OTN	☐ CMW	☐ PCX	☐ HEND	☐ BND	☐ BMUN	☐ CONV	☐ ID	☐ FND	☐ STIC	☐ CGE	☐ SHD				

1 ☐ POSS DUPE ☐ **BUY** ATTN:

2 QUANTITY | SYMBOL OR DESCRIPTION | SUFFIX* | PRICE OR MARKET | STOP ☐ STP | STOP LIMIT PRICE ____ LMT | TYPE OF ORDER OTHER THAN LIMITED OR MARKET ☐ BAS ☐ OB ☐ WITH DISCRETION ☐ WOW ☐ CLO

3 ☐ AON ☐ NH ☐ DAY ☐ GTC ☐ OPG ☐ FOK ☐ OC ☐ DNR ☐ CASH ☐ ND | PRINCIPAL TRANSACTION

4 ☐ POSS DUPE ☐ OR ☐ SW ☐ CXL ☐ BUY | ☐ INFORM CUSTOMER WE MAKE MARKET

5 QUANTITY | SYMBOL OR DESCRIPTION | SUFFIX* | PRICE OR MARKET | STOP ☐ STP | STOP LIMIT PRICE ____ LMT | ☐ BAS ☐ OB ☐ WITH DISCRETION ☐ WOW ☐ CLO

6 LVS ☐ AON ☐ NH ☐ DAY ☐ GTC ☐ OPG ☐ FOK ☐ OC ☐ DNR ☐ CASH ☐ ND ☐ CHECK IF NEW ACCOUNT

7 OFFICE | ACCOUNT NUMBER | TYPE | **TYPE OF ACCOUNT** 0-COD 1-CASH 2-MARGIN 3-SHORT 4-SPEC. SUBSCRIPTION 5-CONV. BOND 6-SPEC. BOND | SPLIT SHARES | DISCRETIONARY NYSE RULE 406 | EMPLOYEE | A.E. NO. | MGR'S APPROVAL

8 CXL'S ONLY | REF | ORIG STATION | MESSAGE NO. | CUSTOMER NAME

9 COM ☐ A.E. OVERRIDE [R/___] ☐ NEG. ¢ PER SH [M/90 ___] ☐ NEG. DISC. [CD__%] ☐ ST INS OVERRIDE [I/_]

10 COM ☐ SPECIAL DESCRIPTIVE INST. [D/______________________________] ☐ D/UNSOL

11 COM

12 COM

13 CONFIRM LINE CFN LINE 2 & 5

SUFFIX CODES

CALLED CL
CERTIFICATE . CT
CLASS OF ..... AB
SECURITY . ETC.
CONVERTIBLE CV
FOREIGN ..... F
PREFERRED ... PR
RIGHTS ..... RT
SPECIAL ..... SP
STAMPED ... SD
WHEN DISTRIBUTED . WD
WHEN ISSUED ... WI
WITH WARRANTS .. WW
WITHOUT WARRANTS . XW
WARRANTS . WS

ORDER COPY

9

S E L L

SUFFIX CODES

- CALLED CL
- CERTIFICATE . CT
- CLASS OF SECURITY . AB ETC.
- CONVERTIBLE CV
- FOREIGN . F
- PREFERRED PR
- RIGHTS RT
- SPECIAL SP
- STAMPED . SD
- WHEN DISTRIBUTED . WD
- WHEN ISSUED . WI
- WITH WARRANTS . WW
- WITHOUT WARRANTS . XW
- WARRANTS . WS

0 STOCK EXCHANGES: NYSE & ASE ☐ NAX; NASDAQ ☐ OTC; OVER THE CNTR ☐ OTN; CHI'GO MID-WEST ☐ CMW; PACIFIC COAST ☐ PCX; BOSTON P-B-W ☐ HEND — BONDS: CORP-ORATE ☐ BND; MUNI-CIPAL ☐ BMUN; CONV-ERTIBLE ☐ CONV — BLOCK DEPT ☐ ID — FINAN SERV DEPT ☐ FND — SYNDI-CATE ☐ STIC — MUTUAL FUNDS ☐ CGE — SPECIAL HAND'NG ☐ SHD — OTHER — ORDER NUMBER — OFFICE — EXECUTED PRICE

1 ☐ POSS DUPE — ☐ **SELL** — ATTN:

2 QUANTITY — SYMBOL OR DESCRIPTION — SUFFIX* — PRICE OR MARKET — STOP ☐ STP — STOP LIMIT PRICE ____ LMT — TYPE OF ORDER OTHER THAN LIMITED OR MARKET: ☐ BAS ☐ OB ☐ WITH DISCRETION ☐ WOW ☐ CLO

3 ☐ AON ☐ NH ☐ DAY ☐ GTC ☐ OPG ☐ FOK ☐ OC ☐ DNR ☐ CASH ☐ ND — PRINCIPAL TRANSACTION

4 ☐ POSS DUPE — ☐ OR ☐ SW ☐ CXL ☐ BUY — ☐ INFORM CUSTOMER WE MAKE MARKET

5 QUANTITY — SYMBOL OR DESCRIPTION — SUFFIX* — PRICE OR MARKET — STOP ☐ STP — STOP LIMIT PRICE ____ LMT — ☐ BAS ☐ OB ☐ WITH DISCRETION ☐ WOW ☐ CLO

6 LVS ☐ AON ☐ NH ☐ DAY ☐ GTC ☐ OPG ☐ FOK ☐ OC ☐ DNR ☐ CASH ☐ ND — ☐ CHECK IF NEW ACCOUNT

7 OFFICE — ACCOUNT NUMBER — TYPE — TYPE OF ACCOUNT (0-COD, 1-CASH, 2-MARGIN, 3-SHORT, 4-SPEC. SUBSCRIPTION, 5-CONV. BOND, 6-SPEC. BOND) — SPLIT SHARES — DISCRETIONARY NYSE RULE 408 — EMPLOYEE — A.E. NO. — MGR'S APPROVAL

8 CXL'S ONLY — REF — ORIG STATION — MESSAGE NO. — CUSTOMER NAME

9 COM ☐ A.E. OVERRIDE [R/___] ☐ NEG. ¢ PER SH [M/90 ___] ☐ NEG. DISC. [CD__%] ☐ ST INS OVERRIDE [I/_]

10 COM ☐ SPECIAL DESCRIPTIVE INST. [D/______________________] ☐ D/UNSOL

11 COM

12 COM

13 CONFIRM LINE CFN LINE 2 & 5

ORDER COPY

10

SELL

	STOCK EXCHANGES						BONDS			BLOCK DEPT	FINAN. SERV DEPT.	SYNDI-CATE	MUTUAL FUNDS	SPECIAL HAND'NG	OTHER	ORDER NUMBER	OFFICE	EXECUTED PRICE
	NYSE & ASE	NASDAQ	OVER THE CNTR	CHI'GO MID-WEST	PACIFIC COAST	BOSTON P-B-W	CORP-ORATE	MUNI-CIPAL	CONV-ERTIBLE									
0	☐ NAX	☐ OTC	☐ OTN	☐ CMW	☐ PCX	☐ HEND	☐ BND	☐ BMUN	☐ CONV	☐ ID	☐ FND	☐ STIC	☐ CGE	☐ SHD				

1 ☐ POSS DUPE ☐ SELL ATTN:

2 QUANTITY | SYMBOL OR DESCRIPTION | SUFFIX* | PRICE OR MARKET | STOP ☐ STP | STOP LIMIT PRICE ____ LMT | TYPE OF ORDER OTHER THAN LIMITED OR MARKET ☐ BAS ☐ OB ☐ WITH DISCRETION ☐ WOW ☐ CLO

3 ☐ AON ☐ N H ☐ DAY ☐ GTC ☐ OPG ☐ FOK ☐ OC ☐ DNR ☐ CASH ☐ ND | PRINCIPAL TRANSACTION

4 ☐ POSS DUPE ☐ OR ☐ SW ☐ CXL ☐ BUY | ☐ INFORM CUSTOMER WE MAKE MARKET

5 QUANTITY | SYMBOL OR DESCRIPTION | SUFFIX* | PRICE OR MARKET | STOP ☐ STP | STOP LIMIT PRICE ____ LMT | ☐ BAS ☐ OB ☐ WITH DISCRETION ☐ WOW ☐ CLO

6 LVS ☐ AON ☐ NH ☐ DAY ☐ GTC ☐ OPG ☐ FOK ☐ OC ☐ DNR ☐ CASH ☐ ND ☐ CHECK IF NEW ACCOUNT

7 OFFICE | ACCOUNT NUMBER | TYPE | TYPE OF ACCOUNT | SPLIT SHARES | DISCRETIONARY NYSE RULE 408 | EMPLOYEE | A.E. NO. | MGR'S APPROVAL

TYPE OF ACCOUNT: 0-COD, 1-CASH, 2-MARGIN, 3-SHORT, 4-SPEC. SUBSCRIPTION, 5-CONV. BOND, 6-SPEC. BOND

8 CXL'S ONLY | REP | ORIG STATION | MESSAGE NO. | CUSTOMER NAME

9 COM ☐ A.E. OVERRIDE [R/ ___] ☐ NEG. ¢ PER SH [M/90 ___] ☐ NEG. DISC. [CD __ %] ☐ ST INS OVERRIDE [I/ _]

10 COM ☐ SPECIAL DESCRIPTIVE INST. [D/ ________________________________] ☐ D/UNSOL

11 COM

12 COM

13 CONFIRM LINE CFN LINE 2 & 5

ORDER COPY

SUFFIX CODES

CALLED CL
CERTIFICATE . CT
CLASS OF SECURITY . AB ETC.
CONVERTIBLE CV
FOREIGN . F
PREFERRED PR
RIGHTS RT
SPECIAL SP
STAMPED .. SD
WHEN DISTRIBUTED . WD
WHEN ISSUED .... WI
WITH WARRANTS .. WW
WITHOUT WARRANTS . XW
WARRANTS . WS

TRUE/FALSE

Questions 11–20 are either true or false. Mark T for true, F for false. (Each question is worth 3 points.)

11. A stop order becomes a market order when the price of the security reaches or trades through the price specified by the customer. ______

12. The processing of an order begins after the broker enters it for a client. ______

13. The order room handles orders for over-the-counter securities only. ______

14. A market order is executed at the current market price. ______

15. To sell at the market, you are willing to accept the lowest bid for your stock. ______

16. In the order room, one of the first functions of the day is to resolve the previous day's problem trades. ______

17. IOC, FOK, AON, and NH orders make up the bulk of the orders handled by the order department. ______

18. A day order may be executed at any time. ______

19. When a problem occurs in the execution of a trade, listed securities transactions are returned to the trader. ______

20. Newly-entered GTC orders require add notices. ______

Answer Sheet

Matching Quiz

3 market order
10 AON order
8 add buy
2 stop order
12 buy at the market
7 specialist firm
5 short sale
1 volatile issue
9 as-of date
4 nothing done

Multiple Choice

1. c
2. a
3. c
4. c
5. e

True/False

11. T
12. F
13. F
14. F
15. F
16. T
17. F
18. F
19. F
20. T

For answers to questions 6–10, see the following forms.

6

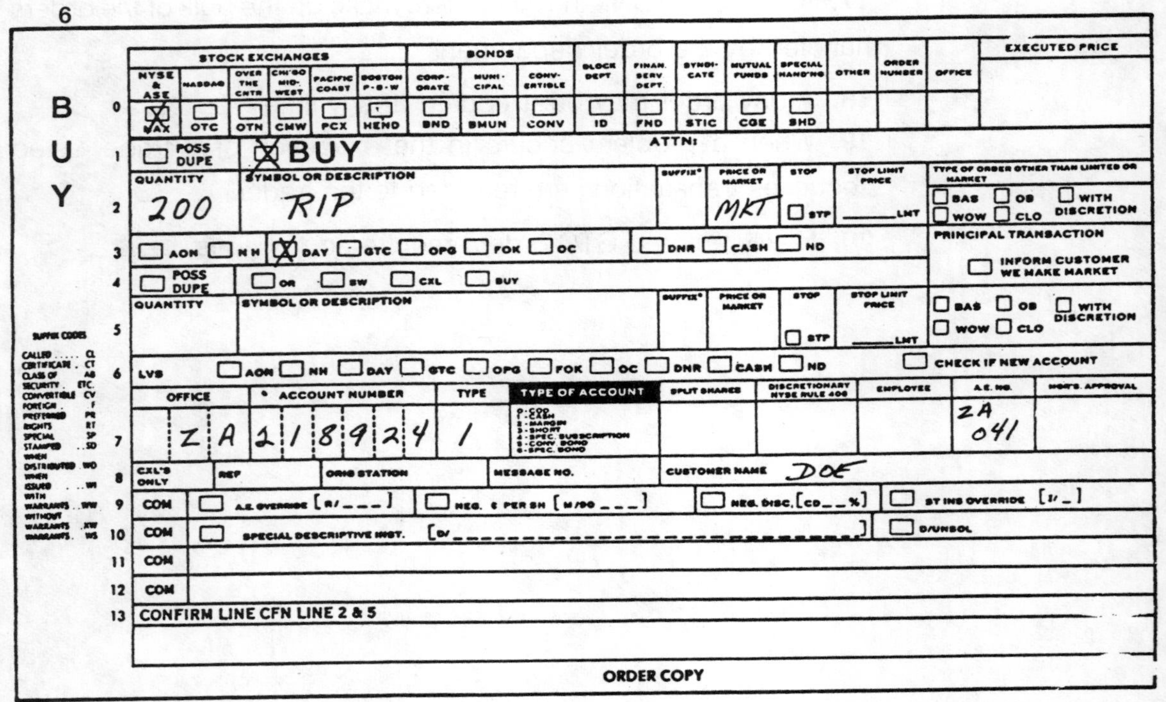

BUY

STOCK EXCHANGES: NYSE & ASE [X] NAX | NASDAQ OTC | OVER THE CNTR OTN | CHI'GO MID-WEST CMW | PACIFIC COAST PCX | BOSTON P-B-W HEND
BONDS: CORP-ORATE BND | MUNI-CIPAL BMUN | CONV-ERTIBLE CONV
BLOCK DEPT ID | FINAN. SERV DEPT. FND | SYNDI-CATE STIC | MUTUAL FUNDS CGE | SPECIAL HAND'NG SHD | OTHER | ORDER NUMBER | OFFICE | EXECUTED PRICE

1 POSS DUPE [X] BUY ATTN:

2 QUANTITY: 200 | SYMBOL OR DESCRIPTION: RIP | SUFFIX | PRICE OR MARKET: MKT | STOP STP | STOP LIMIT PRICE LMT | TYPE OF ORDER OTHER THAN LIMITED OR MARKET: BAS OB WITH DISCRETION WOW CLO

3 AON NH [X] DAY GTC OPG FOK OC | DNR CASH ND | PRINCIPAL TRANSACTION

4 POSS DUPE | OR SW CXL BUY | INFORM CUSTOMER WE MAKE MARKET

5 QUANTITY | SYMBOL OR DESCRIPTION | SUFFIX | PRICE OR MARKET | STOP STP | STOP LIMIT PRICE LMT | BAS OB WITH DISCRETION WOW CLO

6 LVS AON NH DAY GTC OPG FOK OC DNR CASH ND | CHECK IF NEW ACCOUNT

7 OFFICE | ACCOUNT NUMBER: Z A 2 1 8 9 2 4 | TYPE: 1 | TYPE OF ACCOUNT: 0-COD 1-CASH 2-MARGIN 3-SHORT 4-SPEC. SUBSCRIPTION 5-CONV. BOND 6-SPEC. BOND | SPLIT SHARES | DISCRETIONARY NYSE RULE 408 | EMPLOYEE | A.E. NO.: ZA 041 | MGR'S. APPROVAL

8 CXL'S ONLY | REF | ORIG STATION | MESSAGE NO. | CUSTOMER NAME: DOE

9 COM | A.E. OVERRIDE [R/___] | NEG. ¢ PER SH [M/00 ___] | NEG. DISC. [CD__%] | ST INS OVERRIDE [I/_]

10 COM | SPECIAL DESCRIPTIVE INST. [D/ ______] | D/UNSOL

11 COM

12 COM

13 CONFIRM LINE CFN LINE 2 & 5

SUFFIX CODES: CALLED CL, CERTIFICATE CT, CLASS OF AB, SECURITY ETC., CONVERTIBLE CV, FOREIGN F, PREFERRED PR, RIGHTS RT, SPECIAL SP, STAMPED SD, WHEN DISTRIBUTED WD, WHEN ISSUED WI, WITH WARRANTS WW, WITHOUT WARRANTS XW, WARRANTS WS

ORDER COPY

7

BUY

	STOCK EXCHANGES						BONDS			BLOCK DEPT	FINAN SERV DEPT	SYNDI-CATE	MUTUAL FUNDS	SPECIAL HAND'NG	OTHER	ORDER NUMBER	OFFICE	EXECUTED PRICE
	NYSE & ASE	NASDAQ	OVER THE CNTR	CHI'GO MID-WEST	PACIFIC COAST	BOSTON P-B-W	CORP-ORATE	MUNI-CIPAL	CONV-ERTIBLE									
0	☒ NAX	☐ OTC	☐ OTN	☐ CMW	☐ PCX	☐ HEND	☐ BND	☐ BMUN	☐ CONV	☐ ID	☐ FND	☐ STIC	☐ CGE	☐ SHD				

1 ☐ POSS DUPE ☒ BUY ATTN:

2 QUANTITY: 400 | SYMBOL OR DESCRIPTION: RIP | SUFFIX* | PRICE OR MARKET: MKT | STOP ☐ STP | STOP LIMIT PRICE ____ LMT | TYPE OF ORDER OTHER THAN LIMITED OR MARKET: ☐ BAS ☐ OB ☐ WITH DISCRETION ☐ WOW ☐ CLO

3 ☐ AON ☐ NH ☐ DAY ☐ GTC ☐ OPG ☐ FOK ☐ OC ☐ DNR ☐ CASH ☐ ND | PRINCIPAL TRANSACTION

4 ☐ POSS DUPE ☐ OR ☐ SW ☐ CXL ☐ BUY | ☐ INFORM CUSTOMER WE MAKE MARKET

5 QUANTITY | SYMBOL OR DESCRIPTION | SUFFIX* | PRICE OR MARKET | STOP ☐ STP | STOP LIMIT PRICE ____ LMT | ☐ BAS ☐ OB ☐ WITH DISCRETION ☐ WOW ☐ CLO

6 LVS ☐ AON ☐ NH ☐ DAY ☐ GTC ☐ OPG ☐ FOK ☐ OC ☐ DNR ☐ CASH ☐ ND ☐ CHECK IF NEW ACCOUNT

7 OFFICE: Z A | ACCOUNT NUMBER: 2 2 0 3 4 5 | TYPE: 2 | TYPE OF ACCOUNT: 0-COD 1-CASH 2-MARGIN 3-SHORT 4-SPEC. SUBSCRIPTION 5-CONV BOND 6-SPEC. BOND | SPLIT SHARES | DISCRETIONARY NYSE RULE 408 | EMPLOYEE | A.E. NO.: ZA 011 | MGR'S APPROVAL

8 CXL'S ONLY | REF | ORIG STATION | MESSAGE NO. | CUSTOMER NAME: KETTESIN

SUFFIX CODES: CALLED CL; CERTIFICATE CT; CLASS OF SECURITY ETC. AB; CONVERTIBLE CV; FOREIGN F; PREFERRED PR; RIGHTS RT; SPECIAL SP; STAMPED SD; WHEN DISTRIBUTED WD; WHEN ISSUED WI; WITH ...

8

BUY

	STOCK EXCHANGES						BONDS			BLOCK DEPT	FINAN SERV DEPT	SYNDI-CATE	MUTUAL FUNDS	SPECIAL HAND'NG	OTHER	ORDER NUMBER	OFFICE	EXECUTED PRICE
	NYSE & ASE	NASDAQ	OVER THE CNTR	CHI'GO MID-WEST	PACIFIC COAST	BOSTON P-B-W	CORP-ORATE	MUNI-CIPAL	CONV-ERTIBLE									
0	☒ NAX	☐ OTC	☐ OTN	☐ CMW	☐ PCX	☐ HEND	☐ BND	☐ BMUN	☐ CONV	☐ ID	☐ FND	☐ STIC	☐ CGE	☐ SHD				

1 ☐ POSS DUPE ☒ BUY ATTN:

2 QUANTITY: 200 | SYMBOL OR DESCRIPTION: RIP | SUFFIX* | PRICE OR MARKET: 34 | STOP ☐ STP | STOP LIMIT PRICE ____ LMT | TYPE OF ORDER OTHER THAN LIMITED OR MARKET: ☐ BAS ☐ OB ☐ WITH DISCRETION ☐ WOW ☐ CLO

3 ☐ AON ☐ NH ☐ DAY ☐ GTC ☐ OPG ☐ FOK ☐ OC ☐ DNR ☐ CASH ☐ ND | PRINCIPAL TRANSACTION

4 ☐ POSS DUPE ☐ OR ☐ SW ☐ CXL ☐ BUY | ☐ INFORM CUSTOMER WE MAKE MARKET

5 QUANTITY | SYMBOL OR DESCRIPTION | SUFFIX* | PRICE OR MARKET | STOP ☐ STP | STOP LIMIT PRICE ____ LMT | ☐ BAS ☐ OB ☐ WITH DISCRETION ☐ WOW ☐ CLO

6 LVS ☐ AON ☐ NH ☐ DAY ☐ GTC ☐ OPG ☐ FOK ☐ OC ☐ DNR ☐ CASH ☐ ND ☐ CHECK IF NEW ACCOUNT

7 OFFICE: Z A | ACCOUNT NUMBER: 2 4 0 4 9 2 | TYPE: 1 | TYPE OF ACCOUNT: 0-COD 1-CASH 2-MARGIN 3-SHORT 4-SPEC. SUBSCRIPTION 5-CONV BOND 6-SPEC. BOND | SPLIT SHARES | DISCRETIONARY NYSE RULE 408 | EMPLOYEE | A.E. NO.: ZA 041 | MGR'S APPROVAL

8 CXL'S ONLY | REF | ORIG STATION | MESSAGE NO. | CUSTOMER NAME: HILL

9 COM ☐ A.E. OVERRIDE [R/___] ☐ NEG. ¢ PER SH [M/90 ___] ☐ NEG. DISC. [CD__%] ☐ ST INS OVERRIDE [I/_]

SUFFIX CODES: CALLED CL; CERTIFICATE CT; CLASS OF SECURITY ETC. AB; CONVERTIBLE CV; FOREIGN F; PREFERRED PR; RIGHTS RT; SPECIAL SP; STAMPED SD; WHEN DISTRIBUTED WD; WHEN ISSUED WI; WITH WARRANTS WW; WITHOUT WARRANTS ...

BUY

	STOCK EXCHANGES						BONDS			BLOCK DEPT	FINAN SERV DEPT	SYNDI-CATE	MUTUAL FUNDS	SPECIAL HAND'NG	OTHER	ORDER NUMBER	OFFICE	EXECUTED PRICE
	NYSE & ASE	NASDAQ	OVER THE CNTR	CHI'GO MID-WEST	PACIFIC COAST	BOSTON P-B-W	CORP-ORATE	MUNI-CIPAL	CONV-ERTIBLE									
0	☒ NAX	☐ OTC	☐ OTN	☐ CMW	☐ PCX	☐ HEND	☐ BND	☐ BMUN	☐ CONV	☐ ID	☐ FND	☐ STIC	☐ CGE	☐ SHD				

1 ☐ POSS DUPE ☒ BUY ATTN:

2 QUANTITY: 300 | SYMBOL OR DESCRIPTION: RIP | SUFFIX* | PRICE OR MARKET: MKT | STOP ☐ STP | STOP LIMIT PRICE ____ LMT | TYPE OF ORDER OTHER THAN LIMITED OR MARKET: ☐ BAS ☐ OB ☐ WITH DISCRETION ☐ WOW ☐ CLO

3 ☐ AON ☐ NH ☐ DAY ☐ GTC ☐ OPG ☐ FOK ☐ OC ☐ DNR ☐ CASH ☐ ND | PRINCIPAL TRANSACTION

4 ☐ POSS DUPE ☐ OR ☐ SW ☐ CXL ☐ BUY | ☐ INFORM CUSTOMER WE MAKE MARKET

5 QUANTITY | SYMBOL OR DESCRIPTION | SUFFIX* | PRICE OR MARKET | STOP ☐ STP | STOP LIMIT PRICE ____ LMT | ☐ BAS ☐ OB ☐ WITH DISCRETION ☐ WOW ☐ CLO

6 LVS ☐ AON ☐ NH ☐ DAY ☐ GTC ☐ OPG ☐ FOK ☐ OC ☐ DNR ☐ CASH ☐ ND ☐ CHECK IF NEW ACCOUNT

7 OFFICE: Z A | ACCOUNT NUMBER: 2 4 0 4 9 1 | TYPE: 2 | TYPE OF ACCOUNT: 0-COD 1-CASH 2-MARGIN 3-SHORT 4-SPEC. SUBSCRIPTION 5-CONV BOND 6-SPEC. BOND | SPLIT SHARES | DISCRETIONARY NYSE RULE 408 | EMPLOYEE | A.E. NO.: ZA 041 | MGR'S APPROVAL

8 CXL'S ONLY | REF | ORIG STATION | MESSAGE NO. | CUSTOMER NAME: HILL

9 COM ☐ A.E. OVERRIDE [R/___] ☐ NEG. ¢ PER SH [M/90 ___] ☐ NEG. DISC. [CD__%] ☐ ST INS OVERRIDE [I/_]

10 COM ☐ SPECIAL DESCRIPTIVE INST. [D/________________________] ☐ D/UNSOL

11 COM

12 COM

13 CONFIRM LINE CFN LINE 2 & 5

SUFFIX CODES: CALLED CL; CERTIFICATE CT; CLASS OF SECURITY ETC. AB; CONVERTIBLE CV; FOREIGN F; PREFERRED PR; RIGHTS RT; SPECIAL SP; STAMPED SD; WHEN DISTRIBUTED WD; WHEN ISSUED WI; WITH WARRANTS WW; WITHOUT WARRANTS XW; WARRANTS WS

ORDER COPY

9

SELL

	STOCK EXCHANGES						BONDS			BLOCK DEPT	FINAN SERV DEPT	SYNDI-CATE	MUTUAL FUNDS	SPECIAL HAND'NG	OTHER	ORDER NUMBER	OFFICE	EXECUTED PRICE
	NYSE & ASE	NASDAQ	OVER THE CNTR	CHI'GO MID-WEST	PACIFIC COAST	BOSTON P-B-W	CORP-ORATE	MUNI-CIPAL	CONV-ERTIBLE									
0	☐ MAX	☐ OTC	☐ OTN	☐ CMW	☒ PCX	☐ HEND	☐ BND	☐ BMUN	☐ CONV	☒ ID	☐ FND	☐ STIC	☐ CGE	☐ SHD				

1 ☐ POSS DUPE ☒ SELL ATTN:

2 QUANTITY: *25,000* | SYMBOL OR DESCRIPTION: *LMC* | SUFFIX* | PRICE OR MARKET: *27* | STOP ☐ STP | STOP LIMIT PRICE ____ LMT | TYPE OF ORDER OTHER THAN LIMITED OR MARKET: ☐ BAS ☐ OB ☐ WITH DISCRETION ☐ WOW ☐ CLO

3 ☐ AON ☒ NH ☐ DAY ☐ GTC ☐ OPG ☐ FOK ☐ OC ☐ DNR ☐ CASH ☐ ND | PRINCIPAL TRANSACTION

4 ☐ POSS DUPE ☐ OR ☐ SW ☐ CXL ☐ BUY | ☐ INFORM CUSTOMER WE MAKE MARKET

5 QUANTITY | SYMBOL OR DESCRIPTION | SUFFIX* | PRICE OR MARKET | STOP ☐ STP | STOP LIMIT PRICE ____ LMT | ☐ BAS ☐ OB ☐ WITH DISCRETION ☐ WOW ☐ CLO

6 LVS ☐ AON ☐ NH ☐ DAY ☐ GTC ☐ OPG ☐ FOK ☐ OC ☐ DNR ☐ CASH ☐ ND | ☐ CHECK IF NEW ACCOUNT

	OFFICE	ACCOUNT NUMBER	TYPE	TYPE OF ACCOUNT	SPLIT SHARES	DISCRETIONARY NYSE RULE 408	EMPLOYEE	A.E. NO.	MGR'S APPROVAL
7	*ZA*	*220345*	*2*	0-COD 1-CASH 2-MARGIN 3-SHORT 4-SPEC. SUBSCRIPTION 5-CONV BOND 6-SPEC. BOND				*ZA 041*	

8 CXL'S ONLY | REF | ORIG STATION | MESSAGE NO. | CUSTOMER NAME *KETTESIN*

9 COM ☐ A.E. OVERRIDE [R/___] ☐ NEG. ¢ PER SH [M/90 ___] ☐ NEG. DISC. [CD__%] ☐ ST INS OVERRIDE [I/_]

10 COM ☐ SPECIAL DESCRIPTIVE INST. [D/________________] ☐ D/UNSOL

11 COM

12 COM

13 CONFIRM LINE CFN LINE 2 & 5

SUFFIX CODES: CALLED ..... CL; CERTIFICATE . CT; CLASS OF ..... AB; SECURITY ..... ETC.; CONVERTIBLE CV; FOREIGN ..... F; PREFERRED PR; RIGHTS RT; SPECIAL SP; STAMPED .. SD; WHEN DISTRIBUTED WD; WHEN ISSUED ..... WI; WITH WARRANTS .. WW; WITHOUT WARRANTS XW; WARRANTS WS

ORDER COPY

10

SELL

	STOCK EXCHANGES						BONDS			BLOCK DEPT	FINAN SERV DEPT	SYNDI-CATE	MUTUAL FUNDS	SPECIAL HAND'NG	OTHER	ORDER NUMBER	OFFICE	EXECUTED PRICE
	NYSE & ASE	NASDAQ	OVER THE CNTR	CHI'GO MID-WEST	PACIFIC COAST	BOSTON P-B-W	CORP-ORATE	MUNI-CIPAL	CONV-ERTIBLE									
0	☐ MAX	☐ OTC	☐ OTN	☐ CMW	☒ PCX	☐ HEND	☐ BND	☐ BMUN	☐ CONV	☐ ID	☐ FND	☐ STIC	☐ CGE	☐ SHD				

1 ☐ POSS DUPE ☒ SELL ATTN:

2 QUANTITY: *400* | SYMBOL OR DESCRIPTION: *RAC* | SUFFIX* | PRICE OR MARKET | STOP ☐ STP | STOP LIMIT PRICE *30* LMT | TYPE OF ORDER OTHER THAN LIMITED OR MARKET: ☐ BAS ☐ OB ☐ WITH DISCRETION ☐ WOW ☐ CLO

3 ☐ AON ☐ NH ☐ DAY ☒ GTC ☐ OPG ☐ FOK ☐ OC ☐ DNR ☐ CASH ☐ ND | PRINCIPAL TRANSACTION

4 ☐ POSS DUPE ☐ OR ☐ SW ☐ CXL ☐ BUY | ☐ INFORM CUSTOMER WE MAKE MARKET

5 QUANTITY | SYMBOL OR DESCRIPTION | SUFFIX* | PRICE OR MARKET | STOP ☐ STP | STOP LIMIT PRICE ____ LMT | ☐ BAS ☐ OB ☐ WITH DISCRETION ☐ WOW ☐ CLO

6 LVS ☐ AON ☐ NH ☐ DAY ☐ GTC ☐ OPG ☐ FOK ☐ OC ☐ DNR ☐ CASH ☐ ND | ☐ CHECK IF NEW ACCOUNT

	OFFICE	ACCOUNT NUMBER	TYPE	TYPE OF ACCOUNT	SPLIT SHARES	DISCRETIONARY NYSE RULE 408	EMPLOYEE	A.E. NO.	MGR'S APPROVAL
7	*ZA*	*240491*	*2*	0-COD 1-CASH 2-MARGIN 3-SHORT 4-SPEC. SUBSCRIPTION 5-CONV BOND 6-SPEC. BOND				*ZA 041*	

8 CXL'S ONLY | REF | ORIG STATION | MESSAGE NO. | CUSTOMER NAME *HILL*

9 COM ☐ A.E. OVERRIDE [R/___] ☐ NEG. ¢ PER SH [M/90 ___] ☐ NEG. DISC. [CD__%] ☐ ST INS OVERRIDE [I/_]

10 COM ☐ SPECIAL DESCRIPTIVE INST. [D/________________] ☐ D/UNSOL

11 COM

12 COM

13 CONFIRM LINE CFN LINE 2 & 5

SUFFIX CODES: CALLED ..... CL; CERTIFICATE . CT; CLASS OF ..... AB; SECURITY ..... ETC.; CONVERTIBLE CV; FOREIGN ..... F; PREFERRED PR; RIGHTS RT; SPECIAL SP; STAMPED .. SD; WHEN DISTRIBUTED WD; WHEN ISSUED ..... WI; WITH WARRANTS .. WW; WITHOUT WARRANTS XW; WARRANTS WS

ORDER COPY

LESSON FOURTEEN

OTC and Exchange Facilities

READING ASSIGNMENT

Chapter 33 OTC and Exchange Facilities
(review Chapters 3 and 4)

OBJECTIVES

- To understand the difference between the OTC market and the exchanges.
- To follow the interaction of the order room with both the OTC market and the exchanges.

READING ORIENTATION

This chapter and lesson reviews how the *order room* interacts with the *OTC market* and also with the *exchanges* (NYSE and AMEX).

The specifics regarding operational requirements and procedures are discussed for each, specifically, how the order room plays a part in the execution of a trade.

Some of the material has been covered in Lesson 2.

KEY TERMS

AMEX, 261
AMOS, 261
Bond room, 261
Commission-house broker, 260
Dealer's broker, 260
Dealer's entry, 255–257
Dealer's quote, 256–257
DOT, 261
Firm quote, 257
First money, 258
Inside quote, 258
Intermarket-trading system, 261
Mark-down, 258–259
Market maker, 264
Mark-up, 258
Member, 260–261
Member firm, 260
Multitraded security, 262
NASDAQ, 256
Nominal quote, 256–257
NYSE, 260
OBO, 262
Open/close, 264
OTC market, 254–256
PERS, 261
Registered floor trader, 261
Rotation, 262
Specialist, 261
Subject quote, 257
Thin-ness, 259
Two-dollar broker, 261

Challenge

MATCHING QUIZ

Match each term at the left with a definition at the right, by placing the number of the definition in the fill-in space next to the term. There are more definitions than terms. (Each question is worth 3 points.)

_____ **subject quote**

_____ **market maker**

_____ **order book official**

_____ **open/close**

_____ **inside quote**

_____ **first money**

_____ **nominal quote**

_____ **dealer's entry**

_____ **mark-down**

_____ **thin-ness**

1. Informs what effect a trade will have on the principal's position.

2. Gives the instructions to the executing broker.

3. A bid or offer that is subject to verification.

4. Permits dealers to change their quotes.

5. Meant for the execution of a trade between brokerage firms.

6. Infrequency that a particular issue will trade.

7. Difference between the price the broker pays to the customer and what he/she gets from the market maker.

8. Buy and sell for their account and risk, to maintain liquidity in the marketplace.

9. Reveals the best highest bid and lowest offer made by dealers.

10. Quantities greater than a round lot are negotiated.

11. Executes customers' limit orders maintained on the limit order book.

12. Total charge to the customer.

MULTIPLE CHOICE

Select the letter that best answers the numbered question. (Each question is worth 4 points.)

1. "B 10 calls WIP JD = 6" translates into the following:

a) Buy 10 shares of WIP bonds for 6

b) Buy 10 call contracts on WIP preferred at 6

c) Buy 10 call contracts of WIP common stock October 5 for $600 per contract

d) Buy 10 call contracts on WIP common stock July-20s for $600 per contract

e) Buy a 10 lot of WIP expiring in July if the price is above $50

2. A municipal bond order is entered to buy $10,000 N.J. Turnpike 8% FA—2011 at 8.25 basis. The 8.25 in the price column translates into:

a) $8.25

b) $8,250

c) Priced to give a current yield of 8.25 percent

d) Priced to give a yield to maturity of 8.25 percent

e) Priced at (1,000 − 8.25) $991.75

3. One automated order-entry system is called PERS. What does this stand for?

a) Pre-execution reporting system

b) Post-execution reporting system

c) Post-entry reporting system

d) Personal reporting system

e) Post-execution rotation system

4. When clients want to purchase municipal securities, their main concern is with:

a) the particular issue

b) yield, amount, quantity

c) the issue, tax exposure, rate

d) tax exposure, interest, rating

e) tax exposure, bond rating, yield

5. When an order is turned over to traders in the OTC marketplace, they check the dealers' quotes on the NASDAQ terminal. How many levels of quotes does NASDAQ deal with?

a) two
b) three
c) four
d) none
e) many

6. What are over-the-counter trades executed against?

a) market makers
b) traders
c) brokers
d) customers
e) order book officials

7. Every order going to the floor of the CBOE must contain how many pieces of information?

a) 2
b) 4
c) 6
d) 7
e) 8

8. Information required on the CBOE order form is:

a) buy or sell
b) open or close
c) firm name
d) quantity
e) all of the above

9. In the over-the-counter market, what does NASDAQ's dealer's quote show?

a) Permits the dealers to change their quote.

b) Displays each quote and the dealer making the market.

c) Reveals the best highest bid and lowest offer made by dealers.

d) Reveals the price of a trade made between brokerage firms.

e) Displays the price at which a dealer must make a trade.

10. When a customer wants to buy a security in the OTC market, the firm's profit is called:

a) a mark-down

b) interest

c) commission

d) a mark-up

e) first money

TRUE/FALSE

Questions 11-20 are either true or false. Mark T for true, F for false. (Each question is worth 3 points.)

11. The number of shares behind a firm OTC quote is 100 shares. ______

12. The NASDAQ level that permits dealers to change their quotes is level B. ______

13. SF&R traders buy 500 shares at 34½ and mark up the price to the client by a ¼ of a point. The charge to the client will be $25 per 100 shares. ______

14. On the floor of the NYSE, the member that executes orders for other firms is a commission-house broker. ______

15. The automated order-entry and reporting system used by the NYSE equity products is called DOT. ______

16. Listed options are opened for trading each day by a system known as rotation. ______

17. In a basis quote, the bid side is never higher than the offer. ______

18. Through its inception, the CBOE allowed the public to buy and sell the exact same instrument. ______

19. The OTC market is a negotiated market. ______

20. In a listed stock transaction, the customer knows only the total charge. ______

Answer Sheet

Matching Quiz

3 subject quote
8 market maker
11 order book official
1 open/close
5 inside quote
12 first money
9 nominal quote
4 dealer's entry
7 mark-down
6 thin-ness

Multiple Choice

1. d
2. d
3. b
4. e
5. b
6. a
7. d
8. e
9. b
10. d

True/False

11. T
12. F
13. T
14. F
15. T
16. T
17. F
18. T
19. T
20. F

LESSON FIFTEEN

Purchase and Sales

READING ASSIGNMENT

Chapter 34 Purchase and Sales
(review Chapter 7)

OBJECTIVES

- To identify the functions of the P&S department.
- To fill out sample contracts.
- To follow and understand contractual procedures pertaining to this department.

READING ORIENTATION

This lesson covers the intricate details of operation in the *purchase and sales department.* Once an order is entered and executed, the trade must go through a series of steps to its settlement, which occur in this department.

P&S processing is comprised of the following functions: recording, figuration, comparison, and confirmation. Each of these activities is crucial to the proper and accurate settlement of each individual trade.

This material was briefly touched upon in Lesson 3. This lesson however, will cover the subject in much greater detail.

KEY TERMS

Add by seller, 284
Added trade, 279
Added-trade contract, 284–285
Advisory transaction, 279
As-of trade, 289
Blotter code, 269
Booked, 293
Cancel confirmation, 291
Cash settlement, 292
Clearing-house comparison, 284
Commission, 269–270
Compared trade, 279
Comparison, 273–278
Comparison ticket, 290
Contract, 278
CUSIP, 268–269
Dated date, 272
DK notice, 284, 290
Ex-clearing, 291
Factor table, 291
Figuration, 269–273
First money, 269
Flat, 272
Long coupon, 272
Net, 269
Next business day, 292
Open/close, 277
Order match computer system, 281–282
Out trade, 275
Questionable trade, 284
Recording, 268
Regular way contract, 279
Regular way settlement, 292
ROTN, 275
Sending the comparison, 290
Short coupon, 272
Supplemental contract, 279
TBA, 291
Trade correction, 293
Trade number, 269
Uncompared trade, 279
When-issued transaction, 291

Challenge

MATCHING QUIZ

Match each term at the left with a definition at the right, by placing the number of the definition in the fill-in space next to the term. There are more definitions than terms. (Each question is worth 3 points.)

_____ **contract sheet**

_____ **SIAC**

_____ **uncompared trade**

_____ **NYSE**

_____ **advisory trade**

_____ **broker comparison**

_____ **PSE**

_____ **CHC**

_____ **CBOE**

_____ **regular way contract**

1. Your trade detail that an opposing firm doesn't agree with.

2. Data input to an added-trade contract.

3. Opposing firm's details of a trade appearing on your contract sheet.

4. A list prepared by the National Securities Clearing Corporation from data submitted by brokerage firms.

5. A list prepared in the P&S department that gives details of each day's buy and sell trades.

6. Produced on the night of "trade date plus one."

7. Trades are cleared through the Pacific Clearing Corp.

8. Where the NYSE sends options trades for comparison.

9. Where the Chicago Board Option Exchange sends option transactions for comparison.

10. Trades are cleared through the National Securities Clearing Corp.

11. A slip that gives the customer details of her purchase or sale of securities.

12. A ticket used by brokerage firms to compare purchase and sales of securities.

MULTIPLE CHOICE

Select the letter that best answers the numbered question. (Each question is worth 2 points.)

Questions 1–8 involve figuration.

1. SF&R commission rate is 1% of first money. A client buys 100 shares of Park Avenue Corp. at 55. What amount does the client owe on this transaction?

a) $5,500
b) $5,555
c) $555.50
d) $55.00
e) $5,238.50

2. With the SEC fee at $.01 every $300 and the commission schedule as explained in question #1, what would a client selling 100 shares of Park Avenue receive?

a) $5,555.19
b) $5,554.81
c) $5,444.81
d) $555.48
e) $54.81

3. SF&R is a market maker in Delta Corp., traded OTC. The quote is 34¼–¾. A client of SF&R wants to buy 100 shares. SF&R will *mark it up* ½ point. The customer will pay:

a) $3,525
b) $3,475
c) $3,425
d) $3,425 plus commission
e) $3,475 plus commission

4. Refer to question #3. Another customer of SF&R wants to sell 100 Delta at the market. Using a ½-point markdown, what would the client receive?

a) $3,425
b) $3,475
c) $3,375
d) $3,425 less commission
e) $3,475 less commission

5. On trade date May 9, settlement date May 16, a customer of SF&R buys $1,000 Serville Properties 9% FA—2006 at 97. How many days accrued interest must be accounted for?

a) 104
b) 105
c) 16
d) 15
e) 106

6. Assume the customer in question #5 bought $1,000 Serville Properties 9% FA—2006 at 97 with a 45-day accrued interest. What is the dollar sum of interest accrued?

- **a)** $88.88
- **b)** $8.88
- **c)** $112.50
- **d)** $11.25
- **e)** $888.89

7. Another customer of SF&R sells $1,000 Randis Corp. 10% JJ—2006 bonds at 94 with $35.00 accrued interest owed. SF&R charges $50.00 commission. What are the customer's proceeds from the sale?

- **a)** $179
- **b)** $925
- **c)** $1,025
- **d)** $79
- **e)** $975

8. An option customer of SF&R buys 1 put SAT Oct 40 at 3. The cost of this option to the customer will be:

- **a)** $4,000
- **b)** $4,300 plus commission
- **c)** $4,300
- **d)** $300
- **e)** $300 plus commission

Questions 9–11 concern customer confirmations.

9. Which of the following pieces of information does not have to appear on a customer confirmation?

- **a)** trade date
- **b)** execution price
- **c)** opposing firm
- **d)** security description
- **e)** account number of client

10. A trade processed on a day other than its trade date must carry which notation?

a) as-of

b) error trade

c) delayed trade

d) secondary transaction

e) discounted trade

11. A confirmation of a principal transaction will not show which of the following?

a) settlement date

b) commission

c) market of execution

d) transaction quantity

e) capacity firm acted

12. What is the function of an order match computer system?

a) It reports executions to the customer and stores the prices for later entry into NSCC.

b) It tabulates a customer's interest.

c) It balances the broker's books.

d) It reports entries to the stock record department and balances margin accounts.

e) It makes the market bullish.

FILL-IN

Questions 13–24 require you to fill-in the appropriate answer. (Each question is worth 2 points.)

Questions 13–19 involve accrued interest days for a corporate bond transaction. Each transaction is to be treated as a separate and distinct action.

$1,000 RIP 12½ FA1—2006

	TRADE DATE	*NUMBER DAYS OF SETTLEMENT DATE*	*ACCRUED INTEREST*
13.	Feb. 9	Feb. 16	________
14.	Feb. 21	Feb. 28	________
15.	Feb. 22	Mar. 1	________
16.	May 14	May 21	________
17.	Aug. 9	Aug. 16	________
18.	Aug. 24	Aug. 31	________
19.	Aug. 25	Sept. 11	________

Questions 20–24 require you to make entries on an NSCC type regular way contract. Place each entry in the appropriate column(s) (compared, uncompared, or advisory). You are Stone, Forrest & Rivers (SF&R), clearing number 035.

20. Firm #035 submits a trade for a purchase of 100 shares Craigonics at 46½ against #160. Firms 160 agrees to the trade.

21. Firm #035 submits a purchase of 300 shares Lafayette Ltd. at 38 against #590. Firm 590 knows the trade at 38⅛.

22. Firm #035 enters the detail of a purchase of 100 Hanover Leasing at 26 against #335. Firm 335 did not submit against it.

23. Firm #220 submits a sell transaction of 100 Reptile Leather Corp. at 31 against SF&R, #035. SF&R does not know the transaction.

24. Firm #001 submits a sell transaction against #035 for 200 shares Yellow Bee Mines at 7¾. SF&R knows 7⅜.

	COMPARED	UNCOMPARED	ADVISORY
20.	______	______	______
21.	______	______	______
22.	______	______	______
23.	______	______	______
24.	______	______	______

TRUE/FALSE

Questions 25–34 are either true or false. Mark T for true, F for false. (Each question is worth 2 points).

25. ROTNs take place the day before a trade. ______

26. Bonds that trade flat do so with accrued interest. ______

27. First money is the quantity of securities in the trade times the price of execution, without any deductions. ______

28. A supplemental contract is produced on T+2. ______

29. The AMEX comparison cycle uses a QT notice on added trade contracts. ______

30. In the P&S area, trades are figured, processed, compared, and booked. ______

31. In a regular way contract, most securities settle seven business days after the trade date. ______

32. When an order becomes lost, it becomes an as-of trade. ______

33. OCC is the central clearing corporation for all SEC-regulated option transactions. ______

34. Options and futures are compared on the trade date. ______

Answer Sheet

Matching Quiz

4 contract sheet
8 SIAC
1 uncompared trade
10 NYSE
3 advisory trade
12 broker comparison
7 PSE
2 CHC
9 CBOE
6 regular way contract

Fill-In

13. 15
14. 27
15. 30
16. 110
17. 15
18. 30
19. 40
20. Compared 46½
21. Uncompared 38 Advisory 38⅛
22. Uncompared 26
23. Advisory 31
24. Uncompared 7⅜ Advisory 7¾

Multiple Choice

1. d
2. c
3. a
4. c
5. b
6. d
7. b
8. e
9. c
10. a
11. b
12. a

True/False

25. F
26. F
27. T
28. T
29. F
30. T
31. F
32. F
33. T
34. T

LESSON SIXTEEN

Margin

READING ASSIGNMENT

Chapter 35 Margin
(review Chapter 8)

OBJECTIVES

- To understand the complexity of the margin procedure.
- To realize the importance of accuracy within the margin department.
- To be able to compute margin calculations.

READING ORIENTATION

This lesson delves into the complex mathematical calculations that are the crux of the *margin department.* Margin customers must comply with rules and regulations set forth by the Securities and

Exchange Commission and self-regulatory organizations, such as the NYSE. It is up to the margin department to ensure that the rules are being adhered to and to keep track of the customer's account.

The basic function of this department was discussed in Chapter 8. Chapter 35 discusses in detail, referring to specific examples on how the above-mentioned rules come into play.

KEY TERMS

At-the-money, 308
Buying power, 296
Excess equity, 295
In-the-money, 307
Items-due list, 309
Maintenance requirement, 302
Mark to the market, 302
Minimum maintenance margin, 297–298
Original margin, 309
Out-of-the-money, 307
Reg T excess, 295
Restricted account, 304
Special memorandum account, 304
Variation margin, 309

Challenge

MATCHING QUIZ

Match each term at the left with a definition at the right, by placing the number of the definition in the fill-in space next to the term. There are more definitions than terms. (Each question is worth 3 points.)

_____ **equity**

_____ **buying power**

_____ **in-the-money**

_____ **items-due list**

_____ **standard margin**

_____ **Reg T excess**

_____ **SEC**

_____ **minimum equity requirement**

_____ **maintenance requirement**

_____ **restricted account**

1. Informs personnel of monies or securities owed by clients.

2. This increases as market value increases.

3. Minimum equity for a short position at which the customer is called for more money.

4. Enforces rules and regulations with which margin customers must comply.

5. Profitable relationship of the option's strike price and the underlying stock's market price.

6. The deposit of equity on a per-contract basis.

7. Prices of contracts are adjusted to reflect current prices.

8. The amount of stock a client can buy with Reg T excess.

9. Minimum amount of equity that a customer must have in a margin account before the firm can lend money.

10. The amount by which loan value exceeds the debit balance.

11. A rise in market value creates equity.

12. When the amount of equity is between Reg T excess and the minimum maintenance.

MULTIPLE CHOICE

Select the letter that best answers the numbered question. (Each question is worth 4 points.)

Questions 1–7 concern the following account (use a 50 percent margin rate):

Long	*Market Value*
1,000 Digger Mines	30
1,000 Eastern Pacific	25
1,000 High Valley Hardware	40
1,000 IDM Corp.	55
	Debit bal.: $90,000

1. The current condition of this account is that it:

a) has excess
b) is restricted
c) is below maintenance
d) has cash balances
e) must liquidate all positions

2. At what market value would the account go on maintenance call?

a) $30,000
b) $37,500
c) $120,000
d) $127,500
e) $75,000

3. The market value of Eastern Pacific rises to $75 per share, how much excess does the account have?

a) zero
b) $10,000
c) $20,000
d) $25,000
e) $50,000

4. With the account as it is originally presented, the client sells 1,000 shares of Digger Mines at 30. How much of the proceeds of sales can the client remove?

a) zero
b) $15,000
c) $30,000
d) $22,500
e) $7,500

5. With the account as originally presented, if the client sold 1,000 shares High Valley Hardware at 40 and 1,000 shares IDM Corp. at 55, what would the money balance be?

a) $90,000 debit
b) $90,000 credit
c) $5,000 debit
d) $5,000 credit
e) flat

6. With the account as originally stated, the client deposits 1,000 shares of UNEEDUM at $60 per share and 1,000 shares of Underwater Housing Corp. at $75 per share. With these fully paid-for securities in the account, the money balance is:

a) $90,000 debit
b) $210,000 debit
c) zero
d) $45,000 credit
e) $45,000 debit

7. With the securities mentioned in question #6 deposited in the account, how much excess would the account have?

a) zero
b) $285,000
c) $142,500
d) $52,500
e) $500

Questions 8–10 involve the following short account:

SHORT	
100 Rapid Rabbit	60
3,000 Cr	6,000 Cr

8. The customer's equity in the account is:

a) 3,000 Cr
b) 6,000 Cr
c) 9,000 Cr
d) 4,000 Db
e) 3,000 Db

9. If the market value of Rapid Rabbit fell to 50, how much excess would the customer have?

a) zero
b) \$500
c) \$1,500
d) \$2,500
e) \$3,500

10. With the stock at the stated value, to what value could it rise before the firm would have to call for more money?

a) 120
b) 69¼
c) 75½
d) 85¾
e) 50

TRUE/FALSE

Questions 11–20 are either true or false. Mark T for true, F for false. (Each question is worth 3 points).

11. Trades in a cash account must be deposited by the fifth business day. ______

12. An account that records events such as excess or proceeds of sales that the client could have used but didn't, is known as the SMA. ______

13. In computing option margin, a call is in-the-money if the market value of the underlying stock is higher than the exercise price of the option. ______

14. In computing option margin, a put is out-of-the-money if the underlying stock's value is less than the exercise price of the option. ______

15. As a short option position goes from in-the-money to out-of-the-money, its margin requirement will decrease. ______

16. Any margin account can have a credit balance. ______

17. The equity in an account can never be higher than the market value of the stock. ______

18. An account can have a debit balance that is greater than the market value, as long as the equity is not less than ⅓ of the debit balance. ______

19. In futures trading, there are two types of margins: standard and variation. ______

20. A rise in market value enhances a short position. ______

Answer Sheet

Matching Quiz

2 equity
8 buying power
5 in-the-money
1 items-due list
6 standard margin
10 Reg T excess
4 SEC
9 minimum equity requirement
3 maintenance requirement
12 restricted account

Multiple Choice

1. b
2. c
3. b
4. b
5. d
6. a
7. d
8. a
9. c
10. b

True/False

11. F
12. T
13. T
14. F
15. T
16. T
17. T
18. F
19. T
20. F

LESSON SEVENTEEN

Cashiering

READING ASSIGNMENT

Chapter 36 Cashiering
(review Chapter 9)

OBJECTIVES

- To understand how securities are managed by this department.
- To list this department's main responsibilities.
- To know when and under what circumstances the cashier's department becomes involved with operations.

READING ORIENTATION

The *cashiering department* manages the securities and cash that a firm handles in a transaction. Efficiency is critical to minimize the firm's need to borrow and to maximize potential profits.

Detailed scenarios are described in this chapter, and the responsibilities of the cashiering department are discussed. You may recall that general information regarding this department's functions were covered in Lesson 4.

KEY TERMS

Cash on delivery, 318
Cash on receipt, 318
Continuous net settlement, 312–313
Contra, 315
Deliver balance order, 314
Delivery versus payment, 318
Depository Trust Company, 313
Flat, 316
Free, 322
Legal transfers, 323–324
Level 1 exemption, 313
Level 2 exemption, 313
Mainline activities, 314
Next-day money, 317
Parent company, 328
PDQ, 314
Projection report, 312
Receive balance order, 314
Reorganization, 325
Same-day money, 317
Settlement cycle, 311–312
Spin-off, 328
Standing instructions, 324
Tender offer, 328
Transfer agent, 323
Window ticket, 324

Challenge

MATCHING QUIZ

Match each term at the left with a definition at the right, by placing the number of the definition in the fill-in space next to the term. There are more definitions than terms. (Each question is worth 3 points.)

_____ **legal transfer**

_____ **tender offer**

_____ **standing instructions**

_____ **next-day money**

_____ **settlement cycle**

_____ **projection report**

_____ **window ticket**

_____ **free securities**

_____ **DVP**

_____ **flat**

1. Clearing-house funds.

2. Fed funds.

3. Requires legal documentation in addition to the normal forms.

4. Informs the cashiering department of remaining settlement positions.

5. Establishes ongoing procedures which standardize the transfer process.

6. The client pays for purchases upon receipt of the securities and gets paid for sales upon their delivery.

7. Confirms delivery of a certificate to the transfer agent.

8. One firm makes a cash offer for a certain number of shares of another company.

9. Used to cover short sales of other clients.

10. Number of days between trade and settlement dates.

11. Brokerage firm does not have to receive or deliver any securities.

12. Number of days in the post-settlement period.

FILL-IN

Fill-in the answer in the blank space for the following questions. Some configuration may be necessary to obtain an answer. (Each question is worth 2 points.)

Questions 1–6 concern the netting of trades of TIP settling on the same day. The settlement price used by the clearing corporation is $56 per share. The "T" accounts used are as follows.

Bought	Firm (A,B. . .)	Sold
Quantity	Price	
	Price	Quantity

B A S	B B S	B C S	B D S	B E S
100/55	100/56	55/100	56/100	56/100
	57/100	100/57	100/56	
55/100			100/55	

Settlement price: 56

Example: Firm A purchased 100 shares of TIP at 55. The clearing corporation is telling *Firm A* to pay $56 or $100 more than the contract price (55). The clearing corporation would credit (give the) $100 to *Firm A.* On *A's* other trade, the clearing corporation is telling the firm to deliver against a price of $56 or $100 more than the contract price of $55. The clearing corporation would charge *Firm A* (take away) $100. With both trades adjusted to $56 per share, *Firm A* can settle the securities internally.

As explained in the example, what affect would the trades have on Firms B, C, D, and E?

1. Firm B would *receive* or *be charged* $100? ______________

2. Firm C would *receive* or *be charged* $200? ______________

3. Firm D would *receive* or *be charged* $100? ______________

4. What would the effect of the settlement price be on Firm E?

____

5. Which firm would receive an RBO? ______________

6. Which firm would receive a DBO? ____________

Questions 7–10 involve computation of *seg* or free securities at Stone, Forrest, and Rivers.

7. Customer CG 403961 owns 1,000 shares of RAM with a current market value of $56,000. The account has a "zero" money balance (fully paid for). What dollar value of this customer's stock may SF&R use for financing? $________

8. Customer BS 142642 owns 1,000 shares of RAM currently worth $56 per share. The account has a $10,000 debit balance. What is the maximum value of this customer's stock that SF&R can use to finance this balance? $________

9. Customer SF 724361 owns 100 shares of DIP with a value of $60 per share. The account has a $3,000 credit balance. What value of DIP can be used to finance this position? $________

10. Customer SA 824311 owns 100 shares of ZAP worth $25. The account has a $3,000 debit balance. What value of ZAP can the firm use in financing this account? $________

Questions 11–15 concern *seg* requirements of SF&R including securities it has on deposit at DTC, and securities received into its position on settlement date at DTC. The stock is *Marnee Corp.* and SF&R keeps its position in this security at DTC. SF&R has a *seg* requirement of 12,000 shares and has a delivery obligation against settling transactions of 1,000 shares. Based on its total position, how many shares would you release to settle the trades?

	OPENING POSITION	*RECEIVED DURING THE DAY*	*USED FOR DELIVERY*
11.	11,000 shares	0 shares	________
12.	11,000 shares	1,000 shares	________
13.	11,000 shares	1,500 shares	________
14.	11,000 shares	2,000 shares	________
15.	11,000 shares	2,500 shares	________

Questions 16–20 refer to the following scenario:

A tender offer is made by RJW Inc. for the shares of STG Corp. The ratio is one share of RJW Inc. for four shares of STG Corp. held by the owners. Based on SF&R customers' position in STG, how many shares of RJW Inc. would SF&R's reorg department owe each client?

	ACCOUNT #	*SHARES OF STG CORP.*	*SHARES OF RJW INC.*
16.	HT132646	100	____________
17.	AL206145	300	____________
18.	DC300401	60	____________
19.	AT327961	120	____________
20.	M1347961	320	____________

TRUE/FALSE

Questions 21–30 are either true or false. Mark T for true, F for false. (Each question is worth 3 points).

21. The process by which firms pledge securities at a bank to finance margin debit balances is known as hypothecation. ______

22. In lieu of endorsing the stock certificate itself, a stock/bond power may be signed and affixed to the certificate. This attachment would make the certificate negotiable. ______

23. Securities maintained in "street name" must be endorsed by the beneficial owner before it may be used. ______

24. One method of reducing financing costs is through a stock loan. ______

25. The process by which the National Securities Clearing Corporation (NSCC) and Depository Trust Company (DTC) settle transactions on the night before settlement is known as the mainline system. ______

26. Individual instructions must be initiated each time a transfer for a particular customer is needed. ______

27. Ordering certificates is the function of the transfer section of the cashiering department. ______

28. A depository's night cycle is known as PDP. ______

29. When a brokerage firm completes the street-side obligation for its trades, the settlement cycle is nearing its end. ______

30. Two types of transfers are legal and street. ______

Answer Sheet

Matching Quiz

3 legal transfer
8 tender offer
5 standing instructions
1 next-day money
10 settlement cycle
4 projection report
7 window ticket
9 free securities
6 DVP
11 flat

Fill-In

1. Receives
2. Charged
3. Receives
4. Flat
5. Firm D
6. Firm E
7. 0
8. $14,000
9. 0
10. $2,500
11. 0
12. 0
13. 500
14. 1000
15. 1000
16. 25
17. 75
18. 15
19. 30
20. 80

True/False

21. T
22. T
23. F
24. T
25. F
26. T
27. F
28. F
29. T
30. T

LESSON EIGHTEEN

The Stock Record and Accounting Departments

READING ASSIGNMENT

Chapter 37 Stock Record
Chapter 28 Accounting
(review Chapters 10 and 11)

OBJECTIVES

- To understand the format and function of the daily activity run.
- To be able to balance the daily cash record's ledger.
- To identify the reports and statements produced in the accounting department.

READING ORIENTATION

The *stock record department* is responsible for keeping track of the movement of all securities into, out of, and within the brokerage firm. Accuracy and orderliness is of the utmost importance.

The *accounting department* balances money movement entries, utilizing two reports: the *daily cash listing* and the *trial balance.* Customer and street-side money movement are recorded daily and must be accurate or the brokerage firm could lose money. This department also issues checks for services rendered and received.

Lesson 5 covered some of the lighter aspects of these two departments.

KEY TERMS

Activity run, 332
Asset, 342, 348
Balance sheet, 342
Breaks, 336
Expense account, 347
15c3-3 report, 350
Focus report, 349–350
Ledger, 339–340
Liability, 342, 348
Main stock record, 332, 336
Margin excess, 341
Memo fields, 337
Net worth, 342
Profit and loss statement, 342, 346
Revenue account, 347
Revenues, 342
The daily, 332
Trial balance, 346

Challenge

MATCHING QUIZ

Match each term at the left with a definition at the right, by placing the number of the definition in the fill-in space next to the term. There are more definitions than terms. (Each question is worth 2 points.)

_____ **15c3-3 report**

_____ **margin excess**

_____ **main stock record**

_____ **break**

_____ **balance sheet**

_____ **asset**

_____ **memo field**

_____ **P&L statement**

_____ **liability**

_____ **revenue account**

1. Unbalanced entries.

2. Anything owed by the company.

3. Used to locate securities for deliveries and loans.

4. The next day's stock record.

5. Isolates all clients' exposure to the firm.

6. Includes interest income, dividend income, commission revenue, and principal trading profits.

7. Loan value is greater than debit balance.

8. Reports income and expenses over a given period.

9. Report that shows assets, liabilities, and net worth categories.

10. Used to record the organization's earning sources.

11. Anything owned by the company.

12. Shows all accounts for which a position exists on a given day.

FILL-IN

Fill-in the answer in the blank space provided. (Each question is worth 1 point.)

Questions 1–10 involve making entries on an activity stock record. Remember, if a customer position is being adjusted to reflect ownership on SF&R records, it is a debit (LONG). Each corresponding entry to a debit must be a credit (SHORT). Stock going into the vault is a credit, the account from which it came must therefore be debited. (Each question is worth 1 point.)

Example: Account SE602411 brought in 100 shares of ZAP to deposit in the account. The stock was received into the Chicago vault #CGB 5000. Entries would be:

	DEBIT	*CREDIT*
SE602411	100	
CGB5000		100
	100	100

ZAP ACTIVITY STATEMENT	*DEBIT*	*CREDIT*
1. Account BSI02954 bought 100 shares against CNS00000.	________	________
2. A/C BA101021 had 100 shares delivered to their home. The stock was shipped from BSB50000.	________	________
3. A/C CG427971 bought 100 shares against CNS00000.	________	________
4. A/C FW436291 sold 100 shares against CNS00000.	________	________
5. A/C DL547291 brought in 100 shares and it went to firm transfer NYT50000.	________	________
6. 100 shares was taken from NYB50000 and put into customer transfer NYT60000.	________	________
7. The entries in CNS0000 are netted to a single position. This netted position is then reversed (cleaned up) against the firm's position in Depository Trust Co. A/C DTC50000.	________	________
8. 100 shares came back from transfer NYT50000 and were placed in the New York vault NYB50000.	________	________

9. 100 shares were taken from the Chicago vault CGB50000 and used to "clean up" a Fail to Deliver CFD10000. ________ ________

10. 1,000 shares returned from Stock Loan A/C SSL20000 and was sent out on bank Loan SBL30000. ________ ________

Post the entries you made in questions 1–10 against the accounts' previous position and arrive at their new position for questions 11–27. (Each question is worth 1 point.)

	ACCT. #	*PREVIOUS POSITION*	*DEBIT*	*CREDIT*	*NEW POSITION*
11.	BS102954	0			________
12.	BA101021	100 debit			________
13.	CG472971	300 debit			________
14.	FW436291	100 debit			________
15.	DL547291	0			________
16.	BSB50000	100 credit			________
17.	NYB50000	1200 credit			________
18.	NYB50000				________
19.	NYT50000	200 credit			________
20.	NYT50000				________
21.	NYT60000	500 credit			________
22.	CGB50000	200 credit			________
23.	CFD10000	100 debit			________
24.	SSL20000	1000 credit			________
25.	SBL30000	0			________
26.	CNS00000 (Net)	0			________
	CNS00000				
27.	DTC50000	23,000 credit			________

Questions 28–30 are based on the concepts practiced in the previous questions. Establish a main (weekly) stock record using the following positions which involve shares of *Marnee Inc.* in position at SF&R. (Each question is worth 4 points.)

28. Account BSI03456 owns 300 shares, A/C HFI39621 owns 1,000 shares, A/C NY204611 owns 500 shares, A/C DC309411 owns 200 shares, A/C AT314961 owns 500 shares, A/C MI343110 sold short 100 shares, A/C HO527731 owns 600 shares.

29. 1,000 shares are on deposit at Depository Trust Company DTC5000, 500 shares are in the New York Vault NYB5000. SF&R has a Fail to Receive A/C SFR1000, of 300 shares, 400 shares are in "Firm" Transfer NYT5000, 500 shares in Bank Loan NBL1000 and SF&R has a Stock Borrow, NSB1000, of 100 shares.

30. Using break account number 99910156, record the difference between total debits and total credits. If total debits equal total credits, place the #0 next to the account number.

Questions 31–38 concern cash entries to acounts. Though every credit must have an offsetting debit and vice versa, these questions affect only the account mentioned. Check the appropriate column next to each question. (Each question is worth 1 point.)

		DEBIT	CREDIT
31.	A check is deposited into A/C WI509411.	________	________
32.	Interest is charged on the debit balance in A/C FW413417.	________	________
33.	A/C DN504311 sells stocks.	________	________
34.	A/C SD813471 writes an option.	________	________
35.	A/C 624710 receives a cash dividend.	________	________
36.	A/C P0613429 is short stock over a divided record date.	________	________
37.	SF&R accrues commission for its Savannah branch stock brokers SAC2000.	________	________
38.	SF&R's account for money on deposit at First Continental Bank is adjusted to reflect a deposit of Federal Funds.	________	________

Questions 39–45 regard the affect different types of entries have on SF&R's cash account. Answer these questions from the perspective of the cash account. (Each question is worth 1 point.)

	SF&R'S CASH ACCOUNT		
	DEBIT	*CREDIT*	*NONE*
39. A customer deposits funds into his account.	______	______	______
40. SF&R credits A/C BA164971 with a cash dividend.	______	______	______
41. SF&R pays its stock brokers their commission.	______	______	______
42. A/C B0319921 is credited a stock dividend.	______	______	______
43. A/C GA410279 pays SF&R for a purchase on settlement date.	______	______	______
44. SF&R's traders mark to market their long positions which reveals a profit.	______	______	______
45. SF&R pays interest for financing its inventory position.	______	______	______

TRUE/FALSE

Questions 46–58 are either true or false. Mark T for true, F for false. (Each question is worth 2 points).

46. The information in the daily cash record is a summary of SF&R's ledger. ______

47. The importance of the stock record department can easily be understated. ______

48. The daily cash listing records stock transactions. ______

49. Every debit entry must have an equal and offsetting credit entry. ______

50. A balance sheet consists of assets, liabilities, and net worth categories. ______

51. A break in the balancing procedure is a balanced entry. ______

52. The stock record is usually maintained in an account order. ______

53. The account number usually consists of six digits. ______

54. The accounting department must accurately record direct and accrued expenses. ______

55. A profit and loss statement is drawn from the trial balance. ______

56. Commission revenue can be considered an expense account. ______

57. Furniture and fixtures are liabilities. ______

58. The focus report protects customers by isolating all clients' exposure to the firm. ______

Answer Sheet

Matching Quiz

5 15c3-3 report
7 margin excess
12 main stock record
1 break
9 balance sheet
11 asset
3 memo field
8 P&L statement
2 liability
6 revenue account

Fill-In

	Debit	*Credit*
1.	BS102954	CNS00000
2.	BSB50000	BA101021
3.	CG429971	CNS00000
4.	CNS00000	FW436291
5.	DLS47291	NYT50000
6.	NYB50000	NYT60000
7.	CNS50000	DTC50000
8.	NYT50000	NYB50000
9.	CGB50000	CFD10000
10.	SSL20000	SBL30000

	Entry	*Position*
11.	100 Db	100 Db
12.	100 Cr	0
13.	100 Db	400 Db
14.	100 Cr	0
15.	100 Db	100 Db
16.	100 Db	0
17.	100 Db	1,100 Cr
18.	100 Cr	1,200 Cr
19.	100 Cr	300 Cr
20.	100 Db	200 Cr
21.	100 Cr	600 Cr
22.	100 Db	100 Cr
23.	100 Cr	0
24.	1,000 Db	0
25.	1,000 Cr	1,000 Cr
26.	100 Cr 100 Db	
27.	100 Cr	23,100
28.	see correct form	

29. see correct form
30. see correct form
31. credit
32. debit
33. credit
34. credit
35. credit
36. debit
37. credit
38. debit
39. debit
40. none
41. credit
42. none
43. debit
44. none
45. credit

28, 29 & 30.

Account	*Long*	*Short*
BS103456	300	
HF139621	1,000	
NY204611	500	
DC309411	200	
AT314961	500	
M1343110		100
H0527731	600	
DTC50000		1,000
NYB50000		500
NYT50000		400
NBL10000		500
NSB10000	100	
SFR10000		300
99910156		400

True/False

46. T
47. F
48. F
49. T
50. T
51. F
52. F
53. T
54. T
55. T
56. F
57. F
58. F

LESSON NINETEEN

The Dividend, Proxy and New Accounts Departments

READING ASSIGNMENT

Chapter 39 Dividend
Chapter 40 Proxy
Chapter 41 New Accounts (Name & Address)
(review Chapters 12, 13, and 14)

OBJECTIVES

- To understand the complexity and importance of the areas covered in this lesson.
- To know the difference between cash and stock dividends.
- To know what documentation is necessary for each new account.

READING ORIENTATION

When dividends are declared to registered stock owners, the *dividend department* must ensure that the appropriate persons receive the dividend. This can be a very complex procedure if the paperwork is not registered properly. This department must also balance the stock record, as well as handle cash dividends, stock dividends, bonds, and payment of dividends.

The *proxy department* processes all of the material or documentation that stockholders must receive throughout their ownership of a security. This involves the forwarding and processing of proxy statements, and the delivery of annual reports, as well as other printed materials.

The *new accounts department* obtains and maintains all the necessary forms for each account in a firm. Any changes must be made promptly and accurately to ensure proper maintenance of a customer's transactions.

The responsibilities of these departments were also covered in Lessons 5 and 6.

KEY TERMS

Bearer form, 356
Clipping coupons, 356
Cut-off date, 360
Due bill, 355
Ex-dividend date, 354
Full power of attorney, 373
Fully registered, 355, 356
Holders of record, 351
Hypothecation, 364
Lending agreement, 364
Limited power of attorney, 373
Margin agreement, 363
Registered as to principal only, 355
Rights of survivorship, 364
Takeoff, 351–352
Tenants in common, 364
Truth in lending agreement, 364

Challenge

MATCHING QUIZ

Match each term at the left with a definition at the right, by placing the number of the definition in the fill-in space next to the term. There are more definitions than terms. (Each question is worth 2 points.)

_____ **full power of attorney**

_____ **cut-off date**

_____ **hypothecation**

_____ **bearer form**

_____ **takeoff**

_____ **holder of record**

_____ **due bill**

_____ **limited power of attorney**

_____ **truth in lending agreement**

_____ **fully registered**

1. Unrecorded security ownership.

2. When a coupon is removed and surrendered to the paying bank.

3. Enables a person to deposit and withdraw securities or cash, as well as enter orders in the account.

4. Informs clients how the firm computes interest costs on their debit balances.

5. Use of securities as collateral to borrow money from a bank.

6. Interest is paid to the registered owner only.

7. An IOU for stock to be issued on the payable date.

8. The last day to receive proxy votes so they can be counted.

9. Printout obtained by the dividend department.

10. Protects customers by isolating the client's exposure to the firm.

11. Entitles a third party to buy and sell in an account.

12. The person in whose name a bond is registered for principal and interest.

MULTIPLE CHOICE

Select the letter that best answers the numbered question. (Each question is worth 2 points.)

1. Which of the following are involved with record dates?

I. dividend-paying common stock
II. dividend-paying preferred stock
III. corporate bonds
IV. municipal bonds
V. Treasury bonds

a) I only
b) I and II only
c) II, IV, and V
d) I and III only
e) I, III, III, IV, and V

2. The date on which a corporation announces a dividend is known as the:

a) announcement date
b) declaration date
c) record date
d) disclosure date
e) command get it date

3. An account which mandates that a client pay in full buy the fifth business day but not later than the seventh business day is:

a) a cash account
b) a margin account
c) an option account
d) a joint account
e) a partnership account

4. The first day a purchaser of stock is not entitled to receive the dividend is known as the:

- **a)** record date
- **b)** payable date
- **c)** ex-dividend date
- **d)** short payment date
- **e)** Umissit date

5. On stock splits, the ex-dividend date is:

- **a)** four days before record date
- **b)** four days before payable
- **c)** on the payable date or the day after
- **d)** on the record date or the day after
- **e)** set by the corporation

6. The hypothecation part of the margin form permits the firm to:

- **a)** lend money against the market value of the security
- **b)** pledge securities (at a bank) needed to finance the client's debit balance
- **c)** use customer stock to facilitate other clients' short sales
- **d)** transfer and ship client's securities
- **e)** trade options against the client's position

7. In case of the demise of one participant, the form of joint account that transfers the share to the remaining participant is the:

- **a)** joint tenants with right of survivorship
- **b)** tenants in common
- **c)** survivors insurance
- **d)** annuity account
- **e)** annuity joint account

8. The official record date for bond interest payment is:

- **a)** the night before payable date
- **b)** four days before record date
- **c)** four days before payment date
- **d)** the night of payable date
- **e)** four days after dated date

9. The document that states under what circumstance a corporation may conduct a security account is the:

a) charter or by-laws
b) resolution
c) deed of trust
d) board of directors
e) annual report

10. An account is to be operated by other than the principal. This individual is permitted to buy and sell securities only. The individual is said to have:

a) a trust account
b) a margin account
c) limited power of attorney
d) full power of attorney
e) a joint account

11. Which of the following must be completed on a new account form for a retail customer?

I. home address
II. business address
III. social security number
IV. bank reference
V. home and business phone number

a) I, II, and IV
b) I and III
c) I, IV, and V
d) I, II, and III
e) I, II, III, IV, and V

Fill-in the answer in the blank space for the following questions. (Each question is worth 2 points.)

Questions 12–16 refer to the following scenario:

> PIP Inc. is paying a $1.00 per share dividend. Work out the following takeoff sheet from SF&R's record date position. SF&R holds the security for Accounts BA304332 and LA802977 in "customer name" in their vault.

ACCOUNT	*LONG*	*SHORT*
AL103471	300	
AT329431	100	
BA304332	200	
BS129972		100
CG427791	500	
DL503421	300	
DN413422		200
FW403497	100	
HO512996	200	
LA802977	400	
MI329471	100	
SF702311	400	
DTC5000 (Depository)		1,000
NYB5000 (SF&R Vault)		900
NFR1000 (Fail to Receive)		500
NFD1000 (Fail to Deliver)	400	
NSL2000 (Stock Loan)		300

12. The total sum to be receive from the Dividend Disbursing Agent is __________

13. The total sum to be received from DTC is __________

14. The amount being charged against the customer is ________

15. The amount claimed against other firms is __________

16. The amount owed to other firms is __________

Questions 17–20 involve the effect that a cash dividend, stock dividend, stock split, and reverse stock split would have on customer accounts. In the space provided, insert the word INCREASE, DECREASE, or NONE, as it applies to each situation. (Each blank is worth 1 point.)

17. What affect would a $1.25 dividend have on the number of shares in a customer account? __________ On the market value per share of the stock? __________

18. What effect would a 10 percent dividend have on the number of shares long in a customer account? __________ On the market value per share of the stock? __________

19. A 3-for-1 split would have what effect on the shares in a customer's account? __________ On the per share market value of that security? __________

20. A 1-for-10 "reverse" split would have what effect on the shares in a customer account? __________ On the price per share? __________

Questions 21–27 concern a client's relationship with name and address. Which of the following actions would involve the name and address process? (Each question is worth 2 points.)

	DOES	*DOESN'T*
21. A client wants to establish a new cash account.	__________	__________
22. A client wants to switch a position from his account to his wife's and his account (joint account).	__________	__________
23. A client who previously had a cash account wants to establish a margin account.	__________	__________
24. A client has changed her home address.	__________	__________
25. A married client with a joint account has gotten a divorce.	__________	__________
26. A client has died.	__________	__________
27. A client with a margin account wants to buy stock in the cash account.	__________	__________

TRUE/FALSE

Questions 28–40 are either true or false. Mark T for true, F for false. (Each question is worth 2 points).

28. If SF&R maintains their client's stock in SF&R's street name, SF&R has the right to vote. ______

29. Cash dividends are paid on a per share basis. ______

30. The new accounts department verifies the completeness of forms filled out for each account. ______

31. Registered bonds being maintained in SF&R's vault, registered in the name of the customer, will cause the proxies to be sent directly to the customer. ______

32. The proxy department must ensure sufficient proxies are available for their common stockholders whose securities are maintained in street name. ______

33. The margin agreement usually lays out five operational terms. ______

34. Stock dividends for more than 25 percent are handled in the same manner as cash dividends. ______

35. To determine which clients are eligible to vote, the proxy department uses procedures similar to the dividend department. ______

36. Bonds may be owned in either nonregistered or bearer form. ______

37. The first day that a new purchaser is entitled to the cash dividend is called the ex-dividend date. ______

38. Besides clients' voting stock maintained in street name at SF&R, the proxy department is also responsible for its clients' securities physically on deposit at DTC. ______

39. Fully-registered bonds require the same balancing procedure as for stock dividends. ______

40. The new accounts department checks ongoing accounts very infrequently. ______

Answer Sheet

Matching Quiz

3 full power of attorney
8 cut-off date
5 hypothecation
1 bearer form
9 takeoff
12 holder of record
7 due bill
11 limited power of attorney
4 truth in lending agreement
6 fully registered

Multiple Choice

1. e
2. b
3. a
4. c
5. c
6. b
7. a
8. a
9. a
10. c
11. e

Fill-In

12. $300
13. $1,000
14. $300
15. $800
16. $400
17. none/decrease
18. increase/decrease
19. increase/decrease
20. decrease/increase
21. does
22. doesn't
23. does
24. does
25. does
26. does
27. doesn't

True/False

28. F
29. T
30. T
31. F
32. T
33. F
34. F
35. T
36. F
37. F
38. T
39. T
40. F

LESSON TWENTY

Role of the Commercial Bank

READING ASSIGNMENT

Chapter 42 Commercial Banks as a Source of Financing
Chapter 43 The Commercial Bank as Underwriter
Chapter 44 The Commercial Bank as Issuer of Commercial Loans and Paper

OBJECTIVES

- To list the services provided by commercial banks.
- To understand the commercial bank's role as an underwriter.
- To understand the need for and use of commercial paper.

READING ORIENTATION

The required reading for this lesson briefly covers the role of the commercial bank in the issuance of financial services and municipal securities.

Chapter 42 reviews some of the reasons *brokerage firms utilize commercial banks.* They assist in the financing of margin accounts, augment cashiering operations, and obtain same-day money for the brokerage firm.

Municipal securities are brought to market through competitive underwritings, in which commercial banks participate. Chapter 43 discusses how one such bank proceeds to do so.

Chapter 44 covers the *process by which corporations borrow money from commercial banks via commercial paper and loans*.

KEY TERMS

Account of pledge, 382
Cut, 386
Euro CD, 388
Fed fund, 385
Haircut, 379
Interest earned, 380
Interest expense, 380
Lending agreement, 378
Margin agreement, 378
Negotiable CD, 388
Non-negotiable CD, 388
Positive carry, 380
Prime rate, 385
Reserve requirement, 385
Rollover, 388
Selling group, 383
Settled position, 380

Challenge

MATCHING QUIZ

Match each term at the left with a definition at the right, by placing the number of the definition in the fill-in space next to the term. There are more definitions than terms. (Each question is worth 3 points.)

_____ **Fed fund**

_____ **lending agreement**

_____ **haircut**

_____ **interest earned**

_____ **selling group**

_____ **prime rate**

_____ **cut**

_____ **rollover**

_____ **settled position**

_____ **account of pledge**

1. Allows a brokerage firm to pledge a customer's securities at a commercial bank to obtain funds on a loan basis.

2. Assists in the distribution of a newly-issued bond.

3. Reinvestment of funds from a mature instrument into a new one.

4. The percentage taken off the market value of the security for loan purposes.

5. The loanable part of the deposits in a commercial bank.

6. The lowest interest rate at which a bank will lend money to a corporation.

7. Securities are delivered to the bank each evening and picked up each morning by the firm's runners.

8. Securities a firm has paid for and maintains.

9. Permits a brokerage firm to obtain funds from stock loans.

10. Income received on a bond.

11. Issuing commercial paper.

12. When a bank lends money to a brokerage firm and the security has been segregated in the firm's vault.

MULTIPLE CHOICE

Select the letter that best answers the numbered question. (Each question is worth 4 points.)

1. The amount banks can lend to a financial customer's debit balance is based on the maximum firms can use. The maximum is:

- **a)** 100 percent of the debit balance
- **b)** 100 percent of market value
- **c)** 140 percent of the debit balance
- **d)** 140 percent of market value
- **e)** 140 percent of the credit balance

2. Banks will accept collateral against loans via:

- **a)** physical delivery
- **b)** book entry
- **c)** account of pledge
- **d)** all of the above
- **e)** a and b only

3. Commercial banks may participate directly in the underwriting of:

- **a)** common stocks
- **b)** corporate stocks
- **c)** municipal instruments
- **d)** government instruments
- **e)** options

4. Commercial paper is:

- **a)** long-term debt of a bank
- **b)** long-term debt of a corporation
- **c)** long-term debt of a municipality
- **d)** long-term debt of an advertising agency
- **e)** none of the above

5. Commercial paper that is not retired on the due date:

a) is automatically cancelled

b) continues to pay interest

c) ceases to pay interest

d) becomes a corporate note

e) is automatically discounted

6. Each business day, two unrelated factors affect the dollar amount worth of securities maintained on loan. These factors are:

a) market price movement and trading activity

b) interest rates and trading activity

c) trade volume and customer debt

d) market price movement and dividend rates

e) none of the above

7. CDs of relatively large denominations that are traded in the secondary market are called:

a) non-negotiable

b) euro

c) commercial

d) negotiable

e) yankee

8. What is the first step in the issuance of commercial paper?

a) A company in need of funds contacts a broker.

b) A company in need of funds contacts a bank or commercial paper dealer.

c) A company obtains the paper for its own clients.

d) Money is exchanged between the company and the bank.

e) The commercial paper is vaulted.

9. Munis that a commercial bank sells to its customers are sent from the syndicate area to:

- **a)** the vault
- **b)** cashiering department
- **c)** another bank
- **d)** figuration
- **e)** the customer

10. How are securities moved at the depository?

- **a)** manually
- **b)** by book entry
- **c)** via telex
- **d)** theoretically
- **e)** by pledge

TRUE/FALSE

Questions 11–20 are either true or false. Mark T for true, F for false. (Each question is worth 3 points).

11. A corporation that does not qualify for the prime rate has to pay higher interest rates to obtain credibility. ______

12. CDs and commercial paper are issued by the bank for next-day settlement. ______

13. When acquiring commercial paper, the corporation giving the most favorable terms receives the loan. ______

14. Issuing commercial paper is one way for corporations to raise money. ______

15. Brokerage firms may secure a loan with a bank by means of an account of pledge. ______

16. The value of the security is pledged as collateral against the shares themselves. ______

17. When customers' bonds are pledged, the interest belongs to the customers. ______

18. When the interest dollars received on a bond are lower than the interest charged by the bank, the brokerage firm is said to have a positive carry. ______

19. Banks lend a brokerage firm up to 70 percent of an equity's market value and up to 95 percent of a U.S. Treasury's value. ______

20. Physical delivery of municipal bonds is necessary for non-DTC members only. ______

Answer Sheet

Matching Quiz

5 Fed fund
9 lending agreement
4 haircut
10 interest earned
2 selling group
6 prime rate
11 cut
3 rollover
8 settled position
12 account of pledge

Multiple Choice

1. c
2. d
3. c
4. e
5. c
6. a
7. d
8. b
9. d
10. b

True/False

11. F
12. F
13. T
14. T
15. T
16. F
17. T
18. F
19. T
20. T

LESSON TWENTY-ONE

The Commercial Bank and Its Responsibilities

READING ASSIGNMENT

Chapter 45 The Commercial Bank's Role in International Trade
Chapter 46 The Commercial Bank and Cashiering Services
Chapter 47 The Commercial Bank as Dividend Disbursing Agent
Chapter 48 The Commercial Bank as Customer of the Brokerage Firm

OBJECTIVES

- To know why banker's acceptances are used in international trade.
- To understand the importance of and restrictions in the use of the Fed wire.
- To be able to identify the procedures banks use to process securities.

READING ORIENTATION

As we come to the end of the text, *After The Trade Is Made,* the last reading requirement for this course covers the commercial bank and its varying responsibilities. In *international trade,* commercial banks issue banker's acceptances for payment of imported goods, which is briefly discussed in Chapter 45.

Commercial banks have *access to Fed funds* and use these for same-day settlement of securities traded by brokerage firms. Typical procedures for carrying out this activity are covered in Chapter 46.

Chapter 47 talks about the commercial bank's role as the *dividend disbursing agent,* citing examples from one particular corporation.

As a customer of a brokerage firm, the commercial bank has different responsibilities. These are discussed in the final chapter, 48.

KEY TERMS

Affirmation, 393
Banker's acceptance, 389
Bearer form, 397
Delivery versus payment, 392
Don't knows, 394
FAST, 398
Financial institution number system, 393
Institutional delivery, 393
Jumbo certificate, 398
Missed transfer, 395
Receiver versus payment, 392
Receives from banks, 394
Trade acceptance, 389

Challenge

MATCHING QUIZ

Match each term at the left with a definition at the right, by placing the number of the definition in the fill-in space next to the term. There are more definitions than terms. (Each question is worth 3 points.)

_____ **missed transfer**

_____ **banker's acceptance**

_____ **affirmation**

_____ **receiver versus payment**

_____ **receives from banks**

_____ **bearer form**

_____ **jumbo certificate**

_____ **FAST**

_____ **institutional delivery**

_____ **trade acceptance**

1. Method of trade execution via the Institutional Delivery System.

2. Unrecorded security ownership.

3. Fast Automatic Stock Transfer.

4. A brokerage firm does not have the stock properly registered by the night of record date.

5. Trades are settled on a trade-for-trade basis through the Fed wire.

6. Allows for open communication between the brokerage firm and the agent bank prior to settlement.

7. Customer-sold securities.

8. Used in international trade to expedite payment of imported/exported goods.

9. The bank does not recognize the trade submitted.

10. Constitutes acceptance of a trade.

11. Represents most or all of the shares of a given security on deposit at the transfer agent being held for DTC.

12. When a bill of lading is stamped by the brokerage firm's client that imports goods.

FILL-IN

Fill-in the appropriate response in the blank space. (Each question is worth 3 points.)

Questions 1–10 concern commercial bank/brokerage firm interplay. Which of the following affect the relationship between a brokerage firm and a commercial bank?

	DOES	*DOES NOT*
1. SF&R retail client buying a security with cash.	________	________
2. SF&R retail client buying a security on margin.	________	________
3. SF&R trade date position in a security in which it is a market maker.	________	________
4. SF&R settlement date position in a security in which it is a market maker.	________	________
5. SF&R settled position in a security in which it is a market maker.	________	________
6. Security SF&R is using to effect a client's short sale.	________	________
7. As a participant in a corporate underwriting.	________	________
8. As a participant in a municipal underwriting.	________	________
9. In the maintenance of institutional accounts.	________	________
10. In the issuance of banker's acceptances made available for trading.	________	________

MULTIPLE CHOICE

Select the letter that best answers the numbered question. (Each question is worth 2 points.)

11. What happens at the end of a banker's acceptance's life?

a) it is retired
b) the customer's account is credited the amount borrowed
c) the customer's account is credited any accrued interest
d) all of the above
e) none of the above

12. Trust managers at commercial banks must adhere to whose terms at all times?

a) the bank's
b) the customer's
c) the brokerage firm's
d) the DTC
e) the exchange's

13. How does the processing of securities differ between commercial banks and brokerage firms?

a) Banks have access to the Fed wire
b) Banks may issue short-term debt instruments
c) Banks may lend money
d) a only
e) a, b, and c

14. How are trades that are entered into with a commercial bank participant settled?

a) over the counter
b) through the P&S department
c) on a trade-for-trade basis through the Fed wire
d) through the contra-side broker
e) on a market-value basis

15. In a receive versus payment or delivery versus payment type of settlement, the bank acts as custodian for:

a) the customer

b) the brokerage firm

c) the other banks

d) the NYSE

e) the building

TRUE/FALSE

Questions 16–25 are either true or false. Mark T for true, F for false. (Each question is worth 3 points).

16. The commercial bank processes transfers of a security's ownership up to the evening of the settlement date. ______

17. Trades between firms that are customers of a commercial bank (e.g., Banker's First Continental), are considered intra-bank settlements and need not go through the Fed wire. ______

18. The FINS system enables banks and firms to efficiently execute the portfolio manager's buys and sells. ______

19. The coupon on a bond represents payment of six-month interest. ______

20. Bearer bond payments are only made when owners surrender the coupons. ______

21. A communication network between the bank and brokerage firm facilitates next-day trades and inventory control. ______

22. Funds must be cleared on the payable date for the bank to issue dividend payments. ______

23. To facilitate record keeping, many commercial banks close their books approximately two weeks before payable date. ______

24. As transfer agent, the bank is responsible for the timely and accurate recording of security ownership. ______

25. FAST stands for "Fast Affirmation Stock Trading." ______

Answer Sheet

Matching Quiz

4 missed transfer
8 banker's acceptance
10 affirmation
5 receive versus payment
7 receives from banks
2 bearer form
11 jumbo certificate
3 FAST
6 institutional delivery
12 trade acceptance

Fill-In

1. does not
2. does
3. does not
4. does not
5. does
6. does not
7. does not
8. does
9. does
10. does

Multiple Choice

11. d
12. b
13. e
14. c
15. a

True/False

16. F
17. T
18. F
19. T
20. T
21. F
22. T
23. F
24. T
25. F

Final Exam

MATCHING QUIZ

Match each term at the left with a definition at the right, by placing the number of the definition in the fill-in space next to the term. There are more definitions than terms. (Each question is worth 2 points.)

_____ **stop order**

_____ **P&S department**

_____ **supplemental contract**

_____ **loan value**

_____ **excess**

_____ **QT, DK, ROTN**

_____ **market order**

_____ **added-trade contract**

_____ **cashier's department**

_____ **advisory**

_____ **limit order**

_____ **margin department**

_____ **debit balance**

_____ **maintenance**

_____ **GTC order**

_____ **dividend department**

1. Responsible for computation of accrued interest.

2. A trade that you know but the opposing firm doesn't.

3. The listed trade contract containing compared, uncompared, and advisory trades.

4. Sets the highest price for a buy order and the lowest price for a sell order.

5. Memorandum order.

6. Handles reregistration of securities.

7. An order that accepts the best price available.

8. Equity is less than market value.

9. The last set of NSCC contracts for a given trade date.

10. 50 percent of market value.

11. Record date is crucial to this department's responsibilities.

12. The opposing firm's trade that your firm doesn't know.

13. Result of the initial correction process.

14. Remains enforced until executed or cancelled.

15. The loan value is greater than the debit balance.

16. Sets the lowest price for a buy order and the highest price for a sell order.

17. Concerned with Regulation T.

18. Equity equals 25 percent of market value.

MULTIPLE CHOICE

Select the letter that best answers the numbered question. (Each question is worth 1 point.)

1. The form of business which is a legal person under U.S. law is:

- **a)** a proprietorship
- **b)** a partnership
- **c)** a joint account
- **d)** a corporation
- **e)** none of the above

2. Which of the following methods can be used by a corporation to issue common stock shares?

- **a)** underwriting
- **b)** rights offering
- **c)** warrants
- **d)** convertible issues
- **e)** all of the above

3. The document used in a negotiated underwriting by the manager to solicit other firms into the syndicate is a:

- **a)** registration statement
- **b)** red herring
- **c)** final prospectus
- **d)** blue sky form
- **e)** proxy

4. The two main bodies of NASD rules that govern over-the-counter trading firms are:

I. Securities and Exchange Commission
II. Rules of Fair Practice
III. Uniform Practice Code
IV. Rules of Standard Procedures
V. New York Stock Exchange

a) I and IV
b) II and V
c) III and IV
d) II and III
e) I and V

5. The over-the-counter market is considered a:

a) listed market
b) auction market
c) dealer's market
d) unregulated market
e) broker's market

6. Over-the-counter quotes may be:

I. firm
II. subject
III. work-out
IV. size priority
V. specialist priority

a) I and II
b) I and V
c) II, III and IV
d) I, II and III
e) all of the above

7. Some bonds are traded at yield-to-maturity price. Another name for this type of pricing is:

a) dollar pricing
b) yield pricing
c) basis pricing
d) fractional pricing
e) decimal pricing

8. Which of the following are members of the NYSE?

a) commission-house brokers
b) two-dollar brokers
c) specialists
d) registered traders
e) all of the above

9. The method of order execution used for equities on the NYSE is:

a) priority, precedence, parity
b) priority prorata
c) first in, first out
d) largest quantity in, first quantity out
e) all orders are executed at current price

10. The participants of the Chicago Board Options Exchange are:

I. specialists
II. order book officials
III. market makers
IV. brokers
V. all of the above

a) I only
b) I and IV
c) V only
d) II, III and IV
e) I, II and IV

11. ZAP has 5,000,000 shares outstanding and wants to issue 1,000,000 shares more via a pre-emptive rights offering. ZAP is trading at $80 per share cum rights. The subscription price is $74 per share. What is the theoretical value per right?

a) $1.20

b) $1.00

c) $2.00

d) $2.50

e) cannot be determined from information given

12. A customer's confirmation must contain which of the following?

I. settlement price

II. place of execution

III. security name

IV. customer name and address

V. type of account

a) III and IV

b) I, II and IV

c) I, III and IV

d) II, IV and V

e) all of the above

13. On NSCC's regular way contract (trade date + 1), SF&R's trades that the opposing firms do not know appear in which column on SF&R's contract sheet?

a) compared

b) QT

c) uncompared

d) advisory

e) adjustment

14. The department responsible for seeing that for each customer transaction there is an equal and offsetting street-side trade is the:

a) order room

b) P&S

c) margin

d) cashier's

e) stock record

15. The department responsible for the conduct of a customer's account is the:

a) order room
b) P&S
c) margin
d) cashier's
e) stock record

16. The department responsible for ensuring that each debit security movement has an equal and offsetting credit security movement is the:

a) order room
b) P&S
c) margin
d) cashier's
e) stock record

17. The owner of a corporation that has the right to vote is the:

a) common stockholder
b) preferred stockholder
c) bond holder
d) note holder
e) commercial paper holder

18. Long-term corporate debt is known as:

a) participating preferred
b) cumulative preferred
c) common stock
d) callable preferred
e) none of the above

19. Short-term debt instruments of the Federal Government are known as:

a) bills
b) CDs
c) muni notes
d) muni bonds
e) BAs

20. Which of the following instruments usually pay interest on a 365-day basis?

a) corporate bonds

b) municipal bonds

c) U.S. Treasury bonds

d) b and c

e) all of the above

21. The option that permits the owner to sell the underlying security is a:

a) future

b) put

c) call

d) convertible

e) equity

22. The underlying value calculation of equity options is usually:

a) the value of an underlying share of stock

b) one hundred times the value of an underlying share of stock

c) ten times the value of an underlying share of stock

d) different from one equity option to another

e) the premium

23. Short-term debt instruments of corporations are:

a) commercial paper

b) notes

c) bills

d) rights

e) warrants

24. The preferred stock that permits its owner to share in dividends with the common shareholders over and above the preferred stipulated rate is known as:

a) convertible
b) callable
c) participating
d) cumulative
e) straight

25. A share of RAP $8, $100 par value preferred, is convertible into four shares of common stock. If RAP preferred is trading at $80, what would the common stock be trading at to be at parity?

a) $80
b) $40
c) $25
d) $20
e) $100

26. An example of an instrument that pays principal and interest on a monthly basis to its certificate holders is a:

a) preferred stock
b) GNMA
c) convertible bond
d) callable bond
e) right

FILL-IN

Fill-in the answer in the blank space for the following questions. (Each question is worth 1 point.)

Questions 27–33 involve computation of accrued interest days. A client buys 1,000 RAM 12% J&J 2006. (The corporate bond pays interest the first day of January and July.) Given the following trade and settlement dates, how many days of accrued interest would the client owe for each *separate* transaction?

	TRADE DATE	*SETTLEMENT DATE*	*DAYS ACCRUED*
27.	1/14	1/21	________
28.	2/21	2/28	________
29.	2/22	3/01	________
30.	4/09	4/16	________
31.	6/04	6/11	________
32.	6/24	7/01	________
33.	7/19	7/26	________

Questions 34–37 concern the following settling trades of RAM.

FIRM A			*FIRM B*			*FIRM C*		
Bought	PX	Sold	Bought	PX	Sold	Bought	PX	Sold
100	62			62	100	100	62	
	63	100	100	63		62	100	
100	63						63	100

Use a settlement price of 63 to "adjust against" for netting purposes.

34. Firm A would (owe to/receive from) ____________________

the clearing corp. $________ (amount of money).

35. Firm B would (owe to/receive from) ______________________ the clearing corp. $__________.

36. Which firm would be expecting to receive 100 shares? ____

37. Which firm would be expecting to deliver 100 shares? ____

Questions 38–44 concern the following margin account:

LONG	*CMV*
100 Dahl & Co.	$3,200
100 Marnee Sec.	$5,100
100 Randis Ind.	$1,700
100 C.B. Wire Inc.	$2,000
(Use 50 percent margin)	Debit $3,000

38. How much regulation T excess does this account have? $__________

39. What is it's buying power? $__________

40. To what level could the market value fall before you would have to ask for more money? $__________

41. If *Dahl & Co.* rose in value to $6,400, how much of the *customer cash* could the customer withdraw? __________

42. Assuming *Dahl & Co.* rose to $6,400, what would the loan value in the account be? __________

43. Disregarding the results of Question 41 and 42, (the account is as stated above), should the customer sell 100 shares of *Marnee,* what would the new money balance be? $__________

44. Regarding Question 43 and the sale of *Marnee,* what is the buying power in the account after the sale? __________

Questions 45–47 concern the following margin account:

LONG	CMV
100 Eickleberg Ent.	$2,600
100 Rini & Co.	$2,400
100 Solomon Mines	$4,800
100 Sulton Sportsware	$2,200
	Debit $9,000

45. How much regulation T excess does this account have? $__________

46. If the market value fell to $12,000, how much money would you call for? $__________

47. Disregarding Question 46's result, if the market value fell to $10,000, how much money would you call for? __________

Questions 48–52 involve establishing an activity stock record. Make the appropriate entries for RAM.

48. Client BN104211 brings in 100 shares of RAM and it's deposited into the Boston Vault BNB5000.

49. Client DN410311 bought 100 RAM. The stock is in Fail to Receive NFR2000.

50. 100 shares of RAM was removed from the N.Y. Vault NYB5000 and placed into "firm" transfer NYT5000.

51. 300 shares is received into the SF Vault SFB5000 from the dividend agent SDA1000.

52. SE629891 sold 200 shares and it was a CG Fail to Deliver CFD1000.

Use the following form:

ACCOUNT NUMBER	DEBIT	CREDIT

Questions 53–58 involve cash accounting entries. Prepare the cash entries in the following client's account. (Make a single money entry for each.)

ACCOUNT WI429711	DEBIT	CREDIT
53. Bought 100 POP for $8,000	______	______
54. Client pays a check for $4,000	______	______
55. POP pays a $1.00 per share dividend	______	______
56. Sold 300 ROP for $6,000	______	______
57. Client deposits 300 shares of ROP	______	______
58. Final money value is	______	______

TRUE/FALSE

Questions 59–68 are either true or false. Mark T for true, F for false. (Each question is worth 1 point.)

59. Stocks maintained by a firm in customer name are said to be in safekeeping. ______

60. Securities that belong to customers but are maintained in firm name can be used for loan. ______

61. Depository Trust Company (DTC) is a clearing corporation. ______

62. Hypothecation is a process by which firms lend securities to other firms. ______

63. The process by which one day's unsettled trade positions are rolled into the next day's settling positions is known as continuous net settlement. ______

64. To finance debit balances in a client's account, firms may use the client's securities' value up to 140 percent of the debit. ______

65. Stocks registered in joint name and properly endorsed require legal transfer. ____

66. The processing of tender offers is the responsibility of the re-org department. ______

67. On stock splits, the ex-dividend date is on the payable date, or the day after payable date. ______

68. In a JTROS account, the demise of one participant reverts that portion to the survivor. ______

Answer Sheet

Matching Quiz

5 stop order
1 P&S department
13 supplemental contract
10 loan value
15 excess
2 QT, DK, ROTN
7 market order
9 added-trade contract
6 cashier's department
12 advisory
4 limit order
17 margin department
8 debit balance
18 maintenance
14 GTC order
11 dividend department

Multiple Choice

1. d
2. e
3. b
4. d
5. c
6. d
7. c
8. e
9. a
10. d
11. b
12. e
13. c
14. b
15. c
16. e
17. a
18. e
19. a
20. c
21. b
22. b
23. a
24. c
25. d
26. b

Fill-In

27. 20
28. 57
29. 60
30. 105
31. 160
32. 0
33. 25
34. receive from/$100
35. owe/$100
36. A
37. C
38. $3,000
39. $6,000
40. $4,000
42. $0
43. $7,600
44. $2,100 CR
45. $0
46. $0
47. $1,500
48. DN104211 Db BNB50000 Cr
49. DN410311 Db NFR20000 Cr
50. NYB50000 Db NYT50000 Cr
51. SFB50000 Db NYT50000 Cr
52. SG629891 Cr CFD10000 Db
53. debit $8,000
54. credit $4,000
55. credit $100
56. credit $100
57. debit 0/credit 0
58. credit $2,100

True/False

59. T
60. F
61. F
62. F
63. T
64. T
65. F
66. F
67. T
68. T